THE DEVIL'S JIGSAW

by

Barry R. Smith

First published by
INTERNATIONAL SUPPORT MINISTRIES
Pelorus Bridge
Rai Valley   7156
NEW ZEALAND

© Barry Smith Family Evangelism Trust, 1998.

ISBN 0-908961-06-5

Other titles by Barry Smith:
> **Warning**
> **Second Warning**
> **Final Notice**
> **Postscript (P.S.)**
> **Better Than Nostradamus**

For a catalogue of books & videos, write to:
> **International Support Ministries**
> **Pelorus Bridge**
> **Rai Valley   7156,**
> **NEW ZEALAND**

CONTENTS

"Note - **All blackened words and phrases throughout this book are this author's emphases**".

Acknowledgement:
Once again, our grateful thanks to our friend Nic Venter from South Africa for
his wonderful art-work.

PREFACE

The paddle-steamer thrashed its way up the Mississippi River.

It was a beautiful afternoon, and as we were visitors from far away New Zealand, this river excursion was like nothing we had ever experienced before.

Scenes from old movies flashed before our eyes. Honky-tonk music, the smell of liquor, and the air thick with tobacco smoke. Surely, there must be tables surrounded by gamblers all seated with their sleeves rolled up and bar girls looking on.

Our reverie was suddenly disturbed as a small group of friends approached our corner of the room. "Say! We were in attendance at your lecture last night. Would you kindly take the time to recap on your explanation of the seals on the U.S. $1 bill?"

What these men did not tell me at the time was that they were associated with the Freemasons' Lodge, and had difficulty in accepting this society's links to the occult world.

I commenced by pointing to the picture of the Great Pyramid on the reverse side of each note and asked a question that all patriotic Americans should be asking.

Q - "What links does America have with Egypt?"

A - "None at all except in the field of the occult."

FOREWORD

A SUPERNATURAL EXPERIENCE

It began in 1972 on the Pacific Island of Rarotonga. Along with a beautiful singing group of Cook Islanders, we were conducting meetings night by night all around the island.

The tropical sun shone down on this beautiful afternoon up the Takuva'ine Valley situated in the hills just in behind the town of Avarua.

I was on my knees with my Living Bible open at the prophecy of Habakkuk 2:2-3. As I began to read, my whole body began to shake and my tears fell on the open page of my Bible. Prior to this happening, I had been praying desperately to the Lord, to ask His divine assistance on how to reach my fellow countrymen in both New Zealand and Australia. And now, here I was, paralysed under the power of Almighty God, shaking and crying, yet at the very same time, reading the instructions for the days ahead.

And the Lord said to me, *"Write my answer on a billboard, large and clear, so that anyone can read it at a glance and rush to tell the others. But these things I plan won't happen right away. Slowly, steadily, surely, the time approaches when the vision will be fulfilled. If it seems slow, do not despair, for these things will surely come to pass. Just be patient! They will not be overdue a single day!"* [1]

Strangely enough, those words were burned into my spirit, and I didn't have to learn them. I just knew them off by heart.

I finally stumbled to my feet. The answer to my prayer was clear. Write down all the things I had learned so that the readers could rush and tell others. Remember the words - **"slowly, steadily, surely?"** Here we are in 1998. **It is almost fulfilled**. Those who read or listen to the ancient prophecies find them to be 100% accurate.

Over the years it has been our pleasure to assist people in their understanding of current events.

This book, entitled "The Devil's Jigsaw", is the sixth in a series. The enthusiasm of thousands of readers of these books encourages me to write an update as regularly as possible. As we travel around the world lecturing, people meet us at airports, all with the same phrase on their lips, "**It's happening, just as you said**!"

If you do not believe in a super-natural aspect to life, my advice would be to purchase yourself a US$1 bill and try to explain the meaning of the two strange seals on the reverse side of each note, dated post 1933.

These seals may be looked upon as the ultimate challenge for all of the information found in this series. People may try to dismiss the information as absolute nonsense yet the seals and their meanings remain resolute and determined to confront the staunchest unbeliever.

In our last book, "Better Than Nostradamus", we simply outlined the highly secret scheme to set up a One World Government by the year 2000. Herewith is a brief summary of those plans so that you may read this updated book with understanding.

Footnote

[1]   Habakkuk 2:2-3

CHAPTER ONE

A PRECIS FROM OUR LAST BOOK - BETTER THAN NOSTRADAMUS

1. Since time immemorial it has been the aim of certain Luciferian groups to place their master (Satan) on the throne of the world.
2. In the year 1776, on May 1st, an occultist from Bavaria called Adam Weishaupt, set up the Illuminati. (He was nicknamed the 'Human Devil'.) Their aim was to create a New World Order, or a one world government, religion, law system and money system.
3. His plan was to use human rights issues and planned problems, many of them false or concocted, to give the peoples of the world a common cause to fight.

   Six simple ideas were set in motion:

a. **The abolition of the monarchy**. (In 1997, certain forces are working hard in this direction.)
b. **The abolition of national sovereignty**. (In 1997, this is well on its way to completion worldwide.)
c. **The abolition of private property**. (In 1997, New Zealand and other countries are gearing up for this to take place.)
d. **The abolition of inheritance**. (Not yet but the thought is in their evil little minds.)
e. **The abolition of normal family life.** (In 1997, this is here with a vengeance worldwide.)
f. **The abolition of religion.** (In 1997, religious harmony means that each religion must be considered valid. This is difficult for Bible-believing Christians to go along with as Jesus Christ Himself, claimed to be **the 'only way to God'**. Thus, a gradual weakening of beliefs in whatever religion, leads us on to unbelief.)

About the same time the Illuminati was founded, the patriarch of the Rothschild's banking family made a very revealing statement. *"Give me control over a nation's economy, and I care not who writes the laws."*

There is no doubt at all that the old man had the right idea!

Come along, let us use a little intelligent philosophizing.

Q. Name the commodity in this world that excites people to such a degree that they will lie, steal, and kill for it?

A. **Money!**

Wasn't it written somewhere that *"The love of money is the root of all evil."*[1]

The plan was highly complicated and even politicians who are involved in implementing it, are either unaware of it, or show their lack of knowledge by labelling the whole thing - a **conspiracy theory**.

Come on this journey with me and at the conclusion, you will delete the word **theory** and insert the word **facts**.

International Language

The contents of this book are so devastating, that at this point, I felt readers may appreciate some **comic relief**. Some people are asking "Will we ultimately have a new language for citizens of the future Global Village?"

A little item from the Internet should titillate the intellect.

"The European Commission has just announced an agreement whereby English will be the official language rather than German, which was the other possibility. As part of the negotiations, Her Majesty's Government conceded that English spelling had some room for improvement and has accepted a 5 year phase-in plan that would be known as "EuroEnglish".

In the first year, "s" will replace the soft "c". Sertainly, this will make the sivil servants jump with joy. The hard "c" will be dropped in favor of the "k". This should klear up konfusion and keyboards kan have 1 less letter.

There will be growing publik enthusiasm in the sekond year, when the troublesome "ph" will be replaced with the "f". This will make words like "fotograf" 20% shorter.

In the 3rd year, publik akseptanse of the new spelling kan be expekted to reach the stage when more komplikated changes are possible. Governments will enkorage the removal of double letters, which have always ben a deterent to akurate speling. Also, al wil agre that the horible mes of the silent "e"'s in the languag is desgracful, and they should go away.

By the 4th yar, peopl wil be reseptiv to steps such as replasing "th" with "z" and "w" with "v". During ze fifz yar, ze unesesary "o" kan be drpd from vords kontaining "ou" and similar changes vud of kors be aplid to ozer kombinations of leters.

After zis fifz yer, ve vil hav a reli sensibl riten styl. Zer vil be no mor trubls or difikultis and evrivun vil find it ezi tu understand ech ozer.

ZE DREAM VIL FINALI KUM TRU!!"

Footnotes

[1] I Timothy   6:10a

ANNOUNCING THE BIRTH OF THE NEW WORLD
ORDER (WITHOUT GOD), UNDER THE ALL-
SEEING EYE OF SATAN, THE ANTI-CHRIST,
666

CHAPTER TWO

The Plan

Based on the secretly-coded symbols on the reverse side of the US$1 bill, the plan is well on the way to completion. By the way, the seals were designed by the Weishaupt group more than 200 years ago. Please establish these **facts** by reading "Better Than Nostradamus". The seals are not an illusion. You can study them with your own eyes.

Note the eye of Lucifer prominently displayed in the triangle. The Latin words clearly tell us he is setting up a one world system over which he will be in complete control i.e.

> **Annuit Coeptis** (announcing the birth of)
> **Novus Ordo Seclorum** (a secular, heathenistic, new order.)

Some years ago, an audacious fellow challenged me as to the meaning behind these Latin words. He was a nice man but had been taught incorrectly as to the meaning of the word 'seclorum'. At a friend's request, the folk working at the Oxford University library wrote back and told us the true meaning: **"Seclorum** - secular, heathenistic, godless, the absence of God."

Meanwhile, my argumentative acquaintance told me that the eye in the triangle was the eye of Almighty God. (That's cute!)

Almighty God, I can now clearly see, is announcing to the world that He is setting up a secular, heathenistic, godless new order, over which He will have no control. This is not highly intelligent thinking and yet thousands of Freemasons and other non-thinkers around the world have been fed a lie.

In our book "Better Than Nostradamus", we show that the Illuminati is a high masonic degree and they are just one of the groups who are setting up the system.

In 1990/91, at the start of the Gulf War, George Bush broadcast this message to the world. "This is an historic moment. I am hoping the fighting will not go on for long. We have in the last year made great progress in ending the long era of conflict and cold war. We have before us, the opportunity to forge for ourselves and future generations - **A New World Order - where the rule of law governs the conduct of the nations**." End quote. (Emphasis added.)

Mr Bush also spoke about 'a thousand points of light', referring of

"Used by Permission"

course to the other approximately 999 groups who, along with the masonic Illuminati, are busily involved in this project.

The Strategy

1. Destroy the economies of each country by creating large world government lending establishments funded by multi-billionaire private groups, all of them keen on the world government concept.
2. These groups would be headed up by one main bank - B.I.S. (The Bank for International Settlements) in Basle, Switzerland. Next in the line of authority is the G8, then the official lending banks under the control of the G8 would be the I.M.F. and the World Bank.

Let us at this point dispel the 'conspiracy theory' talk, once and for all! New Zealand and Australian Prime Ministers made their biggest mistakes in the year 1961. Now, in the year 1997, we citizens are still paying for it (36 years later).

The **loans** were initially offered at very low interest rates. The two afore-mentioned countries borrowed and borrowed. From that very moment, problems began to arise. We had full employment up to that point in history and no outside country or group threatened either our independence or sovereignty.

The Government borrowed of course, and loaned the money out at very low interest rates. Farmers, rolling in money, had a ball. They carried hay bales around their farms in the back seats of their BMW's and Jaguars.

What the people were not told was that along with the **loans**, politicians also signed **conditions**.

Have you ever wondered why from the year 1984 onwards, these two countries appeared to follow a track of self-destruction?

It was the **conditions** that did it!

Australia - the lucky country - not now!

New Zealand - God's own country - no longer!

Thankfully, some people around the world are beginning to latch onto this information. **It's time others stopped listening to late-night radio talk-back hosts and found out the truth for themselves.**

Anyhow, let us move on, lest we become stuck in the mire of deep political discussion.

3. As a result of these conditions being implemented, both the countries of Australia and New Zealand are now in overseas hands.

That's the good news, comparatively speaking. The bad news is that

the governments of the world are following our example i.e. Russia, Alberta (Canada), Papua New Guinea, the United States of America, Germany, Holland, Greece, Italy, etc etc.

Now - **take notice!**

The countries of South East Asia have been very naughty up to this point.   They wouldn't ask for a loan or accept one.

There was a man who had been married three times. When asked by a friend why this was, he explained - "My first dearly beloved wife died from a dose of arsenic poisoning.
My second dearly beloved wife also died from a dose of arsenic poisoning.
My third dearly beloved wife died from a rap over the skull with a 4x2."
"Why was this?" asked the friend.
"She wouldn't take her arsenic", was the reply.

The whole point of telling that nasty little joke was to illustrate a point. You cannot steal a country's independence and sovereignty until you get them caught in the monetary trap. Metaphorically speaking, each country must 'take their arsenic'.

1997 was the year selected for South-East Asia. A few surreptitious phone-calls in the middle of the night and the collapse was under way. It was very carefully organised!

Proof

Unfortunately for the planners, there are certain people in this world who, like the author of this book, study patterns and catchwords used by these diabolical planners. Sure enough, each media article dealing with the South East Asian meltdown, **foolishly used the same catchwords** that were used on the guinea-pig country of New Zealand.

How then did they go about their nefarious plan?

1. Dig up a scandal or two involving well-known banking or commercial figures.
2. An ill-advised comment by a leading politician can quickly erode **confidence** upon which all banking is based.
3. Result - **capital flight.**
4. Which further results in swift economic collapse.

But wait, who is hiding around the corner smiling like the **wolf** in the story of Little Red Riding Hood?

The Bank for International Settlements (B.I.S.), the G8 and then of course - its 'children', the I.M.F. and the World Bank.

- Please name out loud at this point, your finance minister and central-bank governor. Now, remember, if your country has loans out with the I.M.F., these people have surely met.

Q. What instructions do the I.M.F. give our financial leaders?

A. **Follow the conditions!** This ultimately results in the loss of sovereignty.

The media reports... *"One result of the IMF measures could be trouble in the streets..."* End quote.

Correct! Remember what took place in the streets of Indonesia, May 1998? - Riots!

The **choices** that the I.M.F. offer are very simple:

Work with the I.M.F. and get **wiped out!**

Don't work with the I.M.F. and **be destroyed!**

Therefore, the choice is - be wiped out or destroyed!

Readers, please note that not all who work for the I.M.F. are evil people. Many of them will be shocked when they discover that they are simply tools in the hands of some super-evil conspirators. The same rule applies to the politicians who initially embrace the plan.

In the case of New Zealand, the guinea pig test case country, the two dates to remember are **1984**, the date of the first budget, and **1987**, when the plan was put into operation.

The New Zealand 'Listener' magazine, 19th December 1987, named 5 men who worked on The Plan. It pointed out that *"Rogernomics" was a plan imposed by a small group of ministers on a party which had confused ideas as to what it was letting itself in for..."* End quote.

Christchurch 'Press', 26th June 1987 - *"Mr L.......e admits Rogernomics would never have been implemented had it first been shown to party members....Labour's economic policy had to be sold to the party in various disguises."* End quote. (Emphasis added.)

Later on, as the plan became more vicious and it was obvious that it was apparently treasonous, the Prime Minister of the day, a man with a social conscience, bailed out. Unfortunately, by that time, it was too late. The damage had been done.

Economic sovereignty was gone. Old man Rothschild was correct. Without assets, the government could no longer wield power, and the lie was propagated that **all this selling up would improve efficiency**.

I'm not so sure about the improving of efficiency but I do know my country has been systematically raped by overseas people.

This is all pure fact. Nothing made up or dreamed up by a paranoid author.

Look again, for example, at the statement made by Barber Conable, the President of the World Bank. He visited New Zealand in the late 1980's. *"New Zealand's economic restructuring was a **ROLE MODEL** for other countries which also had to adjust their policies to achieve growth."* End quote. (Emphasis added.)

Author's note - Thank you, Mr Conable. You've been a great help!

A British prisoner of war received a visit from the German doctor.

Doc: "I regret to inform you that the tests have come back regarding the condition of your left arm. It is definitely gangrenous and will require amputation."

Prisoner: "Oh. All right then. Would you just drop it over Liverpool by air, and my old mother can pick it up."

Doc: "We'll see what we can do.

Two weeks later -

Doc: "Very sorry sir, but your right arm is infected. Quick amputation is required."

Prisoner: "Oh, all right then. Just drop it over Liverpool to my old mum. She'll look after it."

Doc: "Okay, we'll try."

Three weeks later -

Doc: "Very sorry but the infection is now in your right leg. We must amputate it quickly."

Prisoner: "Oh, that's all right. Please have it dropped over Liverpool so my mum can look after it."

One month later -

Doc: "Your left leg is now infected. I'm sorry but it will need to come off."

Prisoner: "That's all right. My old mum will be waiting for it. Just drop it over Liverpool, would you?"

Doc: "No, we will not!"

Prisoner: "Why not?"

Doc: "We suspect you are trying to escape!!!"

Gradually, the scene is changing.

Hey! **This is not the end. This is only the beginning!**

CHAPTER THREE

A List of Catchwords for New Zealand - The Guinea Pig

(From 1987 and onwards)

1. <u>Restructuring</u> - Initially six government departments were set aside as prototypes.
   <u>True meaning</u> - Completely destroy the foundations of Government by selling up, little by little, their working tools i.e. **assets.**

2. <u>Redundant</u> - Give many of the workforce a voluntary choice to leave their position. Some receive a golden handshake and leave with a brown paper envelope in their hot little hand. Thus, the workforce is whittled down, not just temporarily, but forever.
   <u>True meaning</u> - **This person has just "got the sack".** Some of those who missed out on the golden handshake became disillusioned. Without any hope of security ahead, they took their own lives.

We chuckled at the variation of terms used in South Africa. Their catchwords are '**Structural Readjustment**'. Should I see a South African leaving his work premises for the last time, tightly clutching his brown paper envelope, I ask him "What has just happened to you?" He answers **"I've just been structurally readjusted"**.

You know, if it wasn't all so serious, it would be downright humorous. Let us continue on with our list of catchwords....

3. <u>Corporatisation</u> - In order that the public do not comprehend what is taking place, construct a large new word in the English language, so that your average citizen will exclaim, "Oh yes, I see". They are improving efficiency by turning the ex-government departments into corporations.
   <u>True meaning</u> - The general public have been fooled again. The aim was not **efficiency** but another step in selling up the sovereignty of the country.

4. <u>Privatisation</u> - The year 1987 continued on when, lo and behold, our next big word appeared. Let us take an intelligent look at this word. How many Kiwi citizens in their right minds would understand what it meant?

Can you imagine them, rushing to their local library and searching diligently through a dictionary to find out its meaning?

Not a chance! They simply believed the lie, that whatever the word really meant, it was all for the best. This word **'efficiency'** was used over and over to condition the peoples' minds.

<u>True meaning</u> - This was the next cunning step in the scheme to sell up the **independence and sovereignty** of the nation. They privatised the corporations so that they could be sold. You will catch on quickly to the plan when you see the next catchword.

5. <u>Shares</u> - Initially only at 49% to overseas people. 51% we are told must remain in our country.

An interesting event may well serve as a good illustration.

During the month of July, 1998, the Auckland International Airport, in New Zealand, floated 51% of its shares on the stock market.

The media made it clear that overseas investors would buy up the majority of these shares, yet, believe it or not, the Prime Minister of New Zealand appeared on television telling us that the aim of the exercise was to encourage New Zealanders to buy these shares.

She later appeared to backtrack a little, and said that of course, New Zealanders may later sell up these shares.

What a stressful job this lady has, endeavouring to serve two masters i.e. the Adam Smith Institute, along with the Mont Pelerin Society, and the electorate in her own country.

In my particular line of work, lecturing around the world on these subjects, I find it unnecessary to attend a comedy play or film as all this devious underhand planning gives me enough laughs. The whole plan is so obvious!

During the year 1997, we included the country of Sri Lanka in our itinerary. I asked the local people for the latest catchword in that country and their reply was '**peoplisation**'. They explained that this word meant that the local people still retained the major shareholding in the ex-government department, and therefore felt secure. Initially, the locals were to have 51% and overseas people - 49%.

Stock Market Hiccups

Readers will possibly recall a strange event that took place in New York and the rest of the world during the latter half of 1997. Remember the old adage - **'When Wall St sneezes, the whole world catches a cold'**.

Now let me ask you a simple question.

Q. When there is a rumour of a stock market collapse, which group hastens to sell up their shares, "just in case"?

a. The experienced overseas stock market dealers?

b. The Johnny-come-lately inexperienced **'peoplisation' type, local people**?

You've got it! **The 'peoplisation' people get a sudden panic attack and sell up their shares.** Who do they sell to? **The secure overseas stock-market dealers**.

We take careful note at the brevity of this seeming crash. 24 hours only - ample time indeed for group 'b' (the peoplisation folk) to cash in their shares and to pick up their money. Meanwhile, group 'a', the experienced overseas investors, smile quietly, as they buy up these shares, add them to their existing 49%. Thus, the ex-government department assets, sometimes called the **'family silver'**, go into overseas hands, never to return again.

I wish all of this was incorrect but sadly, it's true!

6. <u>Repay loans</u> - A lot of money has now been generated. This money now goes back to the I.M.F., the World Bank and other money lenders.

At this point, our country is BROKE - to use a good old-fashioned word. Our overseas debt is lowered, that's all. The result of all this is obvious.

a. **The Government has no money.**

b. **The Government has no assets left to earn money.**

The government members smile and speak to the voters using big words and long sentences.

When involved in television interviews, these leaders of ours are trained to breathe in the middle of a sentence so that they won't have to stop at the end of the sentence. They possibly attend night classes where they are trained to quote such phrases as:

- "The economy as we know it is fully sustainable."
- "The reality is...."
- "When we move into the next phase of our economic reforms, the benefits will be obvious to all."
- "Light at the end of the tunnel...."
- ....and more.

7. <u>Reforms</u> - **Freemarket** reforms, **economic** reforms, **social** reforms, and **industrial** reforms. These words are bandied around by the corrupt schemers who are busily involved in their treasonous trade.

THE ORDER

Antony C. Sutton

322

Wednesday Evening, June 28th, 1882.

I went to the Webster's New World Dictionary for a definition: **Reform - to make better** *by stopping abuses; improve; an improvement; correction of faults.*

<u>True meaning</u> - From what you have read to this stage, surely it is abundantly clear that these dear deluded souls need to be sent a dictionary with a marker in the page under the word '**reforms**'.

I have not met a single person who prefers the country the way it is now, 1997, to the way it used to be pre-1984.

"Woe unto them that call evil good and good evil; that put darkness for light and light for darkness; that put bitter for sweet and sweet for bitter."[1] Written about 740 B.C., this person could have been writing prophetically about the day in which we live.

8. <u>M.M.P - Mixed Member Proportional</u> - In the guinea pig country of New Zealand, once the selling up process was well-advanced, past the point of no return, the public were informed that a new political system was about to be introduced.

This M.M.P. plan would purportedly allow more voices to be heard and thus would prove beneficial to the average voter. **It resulted in chaos**! A coalition. Powerless e.g. Italy, Israel, and now little New Zealand.

The Background

Please understand that these catchwords and plans were not designed in New Zealand. Many groups of planners, involved in 'think-tanks', put their evil minds together to set up this surreptitious scheme.

We shall devote a section to these people a little later in the book.

Yale University in the U.S.A. has within its hallowed halls a highly secret society called '**The Skull and Bones**', or the '**Order**'. It has its roots in Germany and George Bush was a member. These people are fanatically dedicated to the selling out of sovereignty of each nation and the setting up of a one world government.

It follows a philosophy called the 'Hegelian dialectic' after the founder - Hegel.

In the light of this information, you may be asking "Why then do we bother having a Parliament as that has basically been emasculated (symbolically only we trust)?

The answer to this question may be found in Antony Sutton's book - "The Order".

Quote: *"What then is the function of a Parliament or a Congress for*

*Hegelians? These institutions are merely to allow individuals to **feel** that their opinions have some value and to allow a government to take advantage of whatever wisdom the 'peasant' may accidentally demonstrate. As Hegel puts it, "By virtue of this participation, subjective liberty and conceit, with their general opinion (individuals) can show themselves palpably efficacious and enjoy the satisfaction of feeling themselves to count for something..."* End quote.

Please notice also that under the Hegelian system, **the clash of opposites e.g. capitalism and communism must bring about a society neither capitalist or communist. The new synthesis will reflect the concept of the State as God, and the individual as totally subordinate to an all-powerful State.**

CHAPTER FOUR

ANOTHER NAIL IN THE COFFIN!

I like to think of myself as having average intelligence, not overly smart, but on the other hand, not easily fooled. My poor mind struggles with the following questions:

a. If I, a simple New Zealand citizen, can glean all this data, **why can't our leaders in Parliament** learn the same information? **Some of them have over 30 advisors** to assist them with their research.
b. Don't they have children, and in some cases, grandchildren of their own? Don't they mind selling up their national inheritance i.e. the country that they lived in and enjoyed?
c. Has some devil jumped into all their minds? Surely not! But the strange thing is that they are still not satisfied. They've got the bit between their teeth. They're like horses making for water on a dry, hot day.

In writing these books, the reader will notice that I have no time to dwell on personalities. We're all the same in this way. We're born, we live, we die, we all go somewhere which lasts forever and ever. **The problem is, so do our decisions.**

M.A.I.

During the month of October 1997, I received a fax from a very concerned computer consultant. He pointed out that a secret agreement, called M.A.I. (Multilateral Agreement on Investment), was being discussed, not by the Parliament of New Zealand, but by the Cabinet.

"Strange", I murmured to myself, remembering that we are living in strange days indeed.

The heart of this bill, **purportedly** dreamed up by the OECD, a Paris-based international policy organisation made up of 29 rich countries, has proceeded without the knowledge and scrutiny of citizens or elected officials.

Stage II of the Sell Out

As we already know (through reading previous books on the subject), this is a world-wide sell out of national sovereignty, following the New

Zealand guinea-pig experience of 1987. The planners are simply following the three majors planks of Fabian Socialism. One doesn't need to be exceptionally bright to see this:

1. **Plank 1 - Gradualism** - Sneak up on the people with your diabolical restructuring plan. When the time is right, hit hard, and never deviate otherwise all your waiting has been in vain.

Take New Zealand for example - two Ministers of Finance followed these instructions. **Our people asked both to slow down the pace of the reforms. They wouldn't because they couldn't!** They both lost their jobs, but who cares? They served well, and you can be sure that they are presently being adequately looked after by their ??? (shall we call them '**advisors**'?).

2. **Plank 2 - Pauperisation** - Selectively destroy each sector of society using the best methods possible for this deliberate destruction. In the guinea-pig country of New Zealand, 1987 was the real beginning. Each area was attacked. Government workers were sacked, education, health, telecommunications, and energy were restructured, and post offices were closed, farmers, fishermen, meat workers, and seamen on the ferries were affected, phone boxes were changed, not only from red to green in colour, but from coins to cards, and small businesses were ruined. Goods and Services Tax was introduced, leading to small business' filling in up to 36 returns per year instead of three....and the list goes on.

Who thought this up? Was it some little New Zealand man who was given power and authority? Was it all too much for him?

No! His orders were given to him, and along with his four friends, **he simply implemented the plan**, but certainly did not design it. One of the five, the Prime Minister of the day, made it clear that the plan was killing him. He couldn't sleep. Why?

He obviously knew the terrible cost that this diabolical plan was having on his fellow countrymen. The others ploughed on regardless.

What sort of deception is this, that would cause a tiny group of men, without the knowledge of the party that elected them, to destroy - willingly and premeditatedly, their country? The arrogance of it all! Smirking and making clever speeches to cover up their nefarious plans.

And now dear reader, prepare yourself for -

3. **Plank 3 - Dispossession** - Separate the people from the ownership of land and real estate, as ownership gives one a feeling of security. This must be removed at all costs.

Enter **M.A.I. - leaked draft January 1997.**

This horrible treaty is being negotiated behind closed doors. This multilateral agreement will give to **foreign investors** the same rights as local people to bid for assets in this country. These multinational companies will then have unlimited rights of access. **They will control not only our assets, but also our resources.** Our government is now trying to hand over New Zealand's sovereignty to overseas people.

By the way, the penalty for treason used to be hanging. I took note that this penalty was cancelled at a late night sitting of Parliament just before the 'reforms' began in 1987. Can you imagine a line of Cabinet ministers all jerking on the end of ropes outside Parliament?

The overseas investors have only **one aim - profit!** Do you think **we** will be any better off? And some of the politicians still have the gall to speak in favour of this farce!

CHAPTER FIVE

GOODBYE GOVERNMENT - HELLO BUSINESS

The ultimate aims of these evil planners is to:

a. Destroy all small business through over-taxation or rates.

b. Merge all big business until approximately **six companies** control the needs of each country. This is called **centralisation**.

c. These large conglomerates controlled by groups, sometimes called multinationals, will exert enormous economic influence in each country.

d. This will affect employment opportunities (or lack of them) for the middle class people, along with new taxation rates.

e. **Thus, the government of each country is phased out until they become virtually irrelevant**.

Remember again the words of old man Rothschilds - "Control the economy and the lawmakers will fall into line.

Of the 100 largest economies in the world, 51 are corporations and only 49 are countries. Mitsubishi is larger than Indonesia; General Motors is larger than Denmark; Ford is larger than South Africa and Toyota is larger than Norway.

During the year 1995, a behind-closed-doors meeting was held in San Francisco to discuss the global economy of the 21st Century. Present were 500 corporate chiefs, leading politicians and academics.

Shocking News

They decided that with new technology abounding, **only 20% of the world's labour force would be needed. The remaining 80% simply would not be required to keep the world's economy going.** The middle class, as we know it, would shrink dramatically in the rich nations.

Notice now, something which New Zealanders and others are experiencing even now. Because many of the multinationals do not pay tax, or at least, as little as possible, by shifting their incomes off-shore into low tax countries, national government will suffer accordingly.

The people of the guinea pig country of New Zealand understand the words "Wine Box enquiry", where large firms were investigated for shifting large amounts of money across to Rarotonga in the Cook Islands.

ANNOUNCING THE BIRTH OF THE NEW WORLD
ORDER (WITHOUT GOD), UNDER THE ALL-
SEEING EYE OF SATAN, THE ANTI-CHRIST,
666

This, they said, was tax avoidance, and not tax evasion. Guilty or not, the majority of them came out unscathed, to carry on with their interesting style of saving money.

Almost immediately, once the verdict was delivered, a number of those involved immediately sold up their multi-million dollar properties in New Zealand and **moved** overseas. Some went to Australia and others to Switzerland, taking their millions of dollars with them.

Some said it was a case of rats leaving the sinking ship, but I felt this was a little unfair. Some rats choose to go down with the ship.

No Tax for Big Time Aussies

It was recently revealed by the head of the Australian Taxation Office that, *"the vast majority of local and foreign multinationals paid little or no tax in Australia."*

A Serious Question

If ultimately, only 20% of the population is in the work force, how do the majority of 80% get on?

The answer is 'Tittytainment' i.e. a mixture of entertainment, and nourishment from the breasts of the productive minority. As you have possibly realised this is a modern version of the ancient Roman idea of feeding the masses bread and circuses to keep them placated.

Crazy Man, Crazy!

If hundreds and thousands of people were **not** being laid off world wide at this time of writing (December 1997), I would say that this author may require psychiatric assistance. However, it is happening isn't it, even in your country? **People are losing their jobs – millions of them; aren't they?**

The End Result of MAI

Clearly, the instructions have been issued to the New Zealand politicians that, come 1998, or as soon as possible after this year, this country must be opened up for any Tom, Dick or Harry, to buy up the remainder of the shares in services, which most consider should remain part of our national heritage.

The 'Canterbury Farmer', August 1997, suggested a few possible scenarios:

a. A large company such as Nestles could take over the New Zealand Dairy Board.
b. International contractors could take over Christchurch Hospital's Heart Unit.
c. What of New Zealand Post?
d. New Zealand roads could become toll roads.
e. Water supplies could become completely privatised.

All this by the month of May 1998 or as soon as possible after that date.

Open Slather World Wide

Once New Zealanders, the guinea-pig group, have swallowed the bitter pill and become used to it, overseas readers take note, these planners will attack your country in the same manner. Possibly a few catch words will be changed, but we understand the reasons for that, don't we?

Somebody might begin to wake up to the fact that this is a global plan to be hopefully completed by the year 2000.

That was exciting wasn't it? **Now let's turn to the next chapter.**

CHAPTER SIX

GOODBYE TAX HAVENS

Mention the words 'Wine-Box Enquiry' and most New Zealanders will put their hands to their mouths to muffle a yawn. In actuality, the drama was far worse and more wide-spread than most people know.

An investigative reporter, Ian Wishart, wrote a book entitled "**The Paradise Conspiracy**", naming all the big players and exposing what they were up to. Large business firms in New Zealand had been transferring their funds up to the Cook Islands, near Tahiti. Not only **was big business** under investigation, but also the **Government Taxation Department**, and the **Serious Fraud Office**.

Ian Wishart, points out in his excellent book, that among the OECD nations in the Pacific basin, New Zealand's money-laundering laws are among the most lax. The system worked something like this.

At the end of each day, banks and large business firms ended up with a surplus of funds. To cut down on taxation, these funds were deposited overnight in tax-havens and brought back the next day again as paper transactions only. False tax certificates could then be issued and sent back to foreign governments to balance things up. The tax money itself was apparently secretly **paid back under the table.**

The average citizen has not a glimmer of an idea as to the enormity of scams like this one. Big names in the field of business mean nothing to the likes of Joe Bloggs. This New Zealand investigation, concluded after untold dollars had been salted away. Very little happened as a result, apart from some of the main players selling up their multimillion dollar homes and taking the rest of their millions overseas. These characters don't use guns and knives. They use bank accounts and tax certificates.

With massive amounts of money at their disposal, they can hire the very best lawyers and therefore, jail remains a very remote possibility.

Tax Avoidance or Tax Evasion

The difference is that the first one is legal whilst the second one is a criminal offence.

Another interesting question. How do we know that the accused, those being investigated, and the investigators, did not belong to the same secret society and thus protect each other? (For further information please turn quickly to chapter 17.)

Channel Islands Illustration

Some years ago, whilst doing a lecture tour of Jersey and Guernsey, situated between France and England, it was a great joy to meet some of my relatives who were long-time residents of Jersey.

The day before we left the Island, I wished to conduct an experiment. Along with a local resident, we entered a large and well-known bank and were invited in to the accountant's office.

Self: "I am interested in opening an account at your bank."

Accountant: "This should be possible, Sir. I would suggest that an initial deposit of say, 250,000 pounds should be adequate to get things underway."

Being full of faith and enthusiasm in those days, I used my best Oxford-style accent, a la New Zealand, and replied, "Oh, that shouldn't be too difficult", later remembering that I probably had about $2.50 in my bank account back home. The man subsequently handed me the needed papers which had to be filled in and spoke again.

Accountant: "Please remember this, Mr Smith. When you open this account, always bear in mind that your relationship with your own tax department is strictly your business."

Self: "Thank you very much. That is very clear." We then began to leave his office and he called out once more.

Accountant: "Don't forget, will you. Your relationship with your tax department is your own affair!"

Self: "Yes, that's clear. Thank you. Goodbye."

What the man seemed to be saying to me was, "**We are entering into an agreement to rip-off your tax department. If you get caught, don't expect us to come to your assistance**."

Sark

Another little-known Channel Island is the tiny piece of land called 'Sark'. On the 1st October 1997, the European newspaper devoted two full pages to an article entitled *"Isle of the Tax Dodger.*

. . .There is nothing quaint about what is going on in Sark nowadays. The rocky islet with its French place names and its patchwork of dairy farms, has no airstrip and cars are banned. French tourists flock there in summer by ferry from nearby Normandy for the British island's exotic "feudal" appeal and tax free cigarettes.

. . ..The digital phone systems, computers and modems are driving highly

lucrative and controversial off-shore schemes behind the secretive walls of the island's farmhouses earning up to one hundred thousand pounds ($160,000) a year tax-free for residents.

*The ministry has so far **failed to control the mushrooming tax dodges on Sark**......69, is himself the director of large numbers of companies registered in the Isle of Man, the Irish Republic and more exotic jurisdictions such as, the British Virgin Islands in the Caribbean.*

*An investigation has revealed an international **network of high-tech tax-dodging** centred on the tiny island costing European governments millions of pounds in lost tax. Behind the door of a single greenhouse tucked away in a paddock, we discovered telephone links stretching round the world.*

***Many of the "inhabitants" of this 3.2 kilometre-long island are bogus residents.** They have listed addresses and phone numbers, which reach a bank of remotely accessed answering machines or are automatically diverted to destinations in England, or much farther afield, in Austria, Spain, Switzerland, California, even Latvia.*

*More than 200 individuals and companies, swelling the island's true population by 50 per cent - include Belgians, Dutch, Swedes and British nationals **only pretending to live there to take advantage of zero taxes.***

Meanwhile, we have established that of the 400 or so genuine Sarkese who live in this anachronistic semi-independent state, about 40 per cent are also company directors. Many are selling their names as sham nominee "directors" of foreign tax-dodging companies. One single enterprising Sark citizen is a director of no fewer than 2400 companies - beating the existing record out of sight and thousands of such companies are being constantly registered. We have already traced 23,000 purported Sark companies - there are likely to be many others. Such companies, whose true owners are concealed behind the names of Sark "directors" have recently been discovered to be involved in arms smuggling, telephone pornography, a collapsed-metal buying scheme and other attempts to solicit money from investors.

...Peter Crook, director general of the Guernsey Financial Services Commission, is scathing. Describing Sark as "a pimple", "It has got to end. We are not happy with some of the publicity."

...The directors themselves rapidly resign if their companies get into trouble.

...The main attraction of Sark nominee directors to company operators is that, while avoiding tax, they also achieve secrecy.

...Sark has no corporation tax and no company law.

...Asked if the majority of nominee directorship schemes were not designed legally to avoid paying tax, Beaumont said, "I'm sure you're right. That's what the whole finance industry in the entire Channel Islands is all about." End quote.

Keep reading. We have news for all money-manipulators and tax-dodgers. This news, by the way, is not the best!

CHAPTER SEVEN

CHAIN OF COMMAND

During his initial Gulf War speech, President George Bush, a member of a highly secret society called **The Order**, not only spoke of a **New World Order**, but also of a **1000 points of light**.

<u>Meaning</u> - Without the knowledge of the masses of people world-wide, there are approximately 1000 different groups involved in **changing the whole social and economic structure by the year 2000**.

<u>Illustration</u> - If you, as an inventor, wish to build a prototype of your invention, **you do not build all the parts in the same building**. The reason for this is clear. Someone else will soon latch onto what you are up to and will try to put a stop to it, or steal it, before you have had time to patent it.

For this reason, this 1000 groups of restructuring planners stagger their operations world-wide so that hopefully, nobody will realise too quickly what they are up to.

<u>Problem</u> - Any world traveller who knows what he is looking for, will very rapidly put one and one together.

As I travel on planes to the next country and venue, it has been my custom to carry a little cutter in my pocket. Any little article in any publication that has relevance to this subject, I collect. Woe betide the person sitting next to me on the plane who wants to read the paper after me. It is very amusing to see their eyes peering through the holes in the paper where the articles used to be.

Also, we receive piles and piles of clippings from publications all over the world. Friends, listeners and readers, all assist in this great **clue gathering** task.

The whole exercise is quite bizarre really!

It has been fun over the years finding out all these things however, **the message of hope that we present along with the jigsaw puzzle results in many changed lives of both individuals and families.**

When people finally realise that we are talking **sense and not claptrap, facts and not theories**, this, in many cases, acts as the catalyst to re-examine their lives and get them into order, not only with their fellow man, but also with Almighty God.

Face it - things are winding down and there is nothing you can do to stop it!

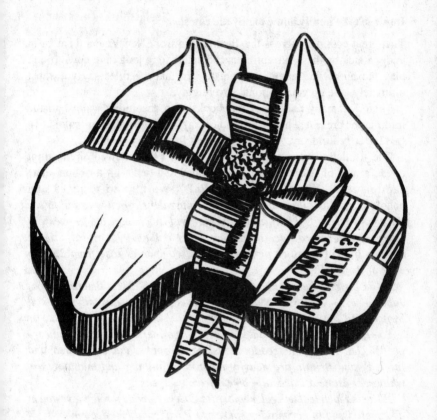

CHAPTER EIGHT

GOODBYE AUSSIE

Don't sell the family home to pay the rates!

That great continent across the Tasman Sea from New Zealand has been under attack by these surreptitious characters for a long time now. If you play the borrowing game, you must learn that the rules say you must ultimately give up your national sovereignty.

There are many readers of our books who absolutely wallow in the information presented here whilst others say **"This guy is a fruitcake". To this latter group I say, "Prepare yourself for a nasty shock."**

The 'Bulletin' magazine, dated 5th August 1987, showed on the front cover, a map of Australia, all gift-wrapped and tied with a ribbon. The caption read *'Who Owns Australia?'* We turn to page 15 and behold........ *"Australians dreaming of owning their own homes fail to see the country being sold off around them - and it is being sold to overseas investors at a record rate. In the four years to July 1996, overall foreign ownership of Australia's publically listed companies rose from 25% to 30% of the total.*

*...The biggest stakeholder is the United States - 23%, Britain - 20%, Japan - 13%, The Netherlands - 3%, Belgium and Luxembourg 2%, Switzerland 2% - **total - 63%.***

Some industries are dominated by overseas owners. The funeral industry is 50% U.S. owned, the feed lot industry is strongly Japanese-owned, and the U.S. and Britain are heavily involved in mining and manufacture, while real-estate attracts all-comers from overseas...

...The independent federal member for Oxley......made foreign investment a keynote issue in her maiden speech to Parliament last September...

"Anyone with any business sense knows that you don't sell off your assets, especially when they are making money."...." End quote.

Please recognise that this lady was the only person in power who made a sensible statement in this regard. However, she had a problem which afflicts most people in the world today, unfortunately including politicians, she simply did not take into account the **IMF conditions**.

I mean, come on, let's be sensible. **What person in their right mind is going to sell up a money-making asset, without any reason to do so?** Have I proved my point yet? Please tick the appropriate square -

$$\boxed{} \text{ Yes} \qquad \boxed{} \text{ No}$$

For those who ticked the 'No' box, please continue to read on. Your excitement will increase to fever pitch, I promise you.

Goodbye Greece

How is this for a headline? 'The European', 28th October 1997 - *"Greece for sale - this time they mean it.*

The Greek national economy minister chose last week's IMF meeting in Hong Kong to announce the revival of the country's stalled privatisation programme.

...told bankers up to 15 companies will be privatised.

...The key utilities such as power are attractive to overseas investors, but not, say some bankers, as promising as Olympics-related franchises. The Greek government plans to set up a private company to operate and finance the Games...." End quote.

The areas to be targeted were listed in this article as:

a. Public Power Corporation
b. The National Gas Corporation
c. The National Water Co
d. Olympic Airlines
e. The National Lottery and Footballs Pools
f. The Public Petroleum Corporation
g. Five Banks
h. Railways
i. Shipbuilding
j. Tourism
k. Mining

Special note - The first areas to be sold off in each country are <u>always</u> **telecommunications and power sources** i.e. electricity, gas, etc.

Remember the Kissinger statement:

By controlling energy, we can control nations
By controlling food, we can control individuals

Goodbye Italy

The next giant headline screamed at us from the 'European' newspaper, 18-24 September 1997 is : *"Italy seeks sale of the century.*

....director-general of the Istituto per la Ricostruzione Industriale (IRI)

set up by Mussolini in 1933 last week detailed for the first time how he plans to sell the companies held by the monster conglomerate by the year 2000.

*... "**We plan to sell everything** over the next 3 years," he confidently told reporters.*

...Banca di Roma will be the first to go in November.

...In December....aims to sell IRI's 86% share in the motorway network, Autostrade, as well as Italia di Navigazione and Lloyds Trieste, Alitalia, Aeroporti di Roma (ADR), Finmeccanica, IRI's defence, aerospace, automation, energy and transport giant will be split up before a sell-off.

*...**Telecom Italia** group is now scheduled to be privatised in October. Enel - 100% of this **electricity company**.*

A remaining 51% stake in oil and gas giant ENI.

100% stake in Banca Nazionale del Lavoro..." End quote.

There it is again you see - the same pattern. Telecom and power, telecom and power. Always the first to go.

Q. Why is Telecom always one of the first to go?

A. **A global dossier is being prepared** on every citizen in the world. Instant access to each file is essential for quick and thorough control over each person from the cradle to the grave.

Who is selling up Telecommunications in Europe?

The 'European', 25 September-1 October 1997 - *"Buying telecom's shares in Europe is becoming almost as easy as picking up a phone. Six telecom companies (possibly 7) are scheduled to issue more than $25 billion in equity over the next 12 months....German Deutsche Telekom, Telecom Italia - merged with Stet, Portugal Telecom, France Telecom, Tele Danmark, Swiss Telecom, Turk Telecom."* End quote.

CHAPTER NINE

THE PLANNERS

Oftentimes I have heard the comment, "They are organising all this!" **Who are they?** Within the pages of this book, you will find very precise information including cunningly concealed hints from the mouths of some of the participating players.

We outlined some of the groups involved earlier in this book. However, here is further detailed information.

Jigsaw piece 1 - One New Zealand politician initially involved in restructuring the guinea pig country of New Zealand made the following statement in Parliament on the 16ᵗʰ July 1981 - *"We will not be able to tackle these problems unless we are prepared to cooperate and **give up some of our national sovereignty**..."* (R......d P.......e). End quote.

His prediction came to pass and strangely enough, this man,.........still strides the halls of Parliament in 1998. (See also page 44 in our other book – "Final Notice".)

Some years ago, selling out one's country to a foreign power would have been called "treason" and we all know the ancient penalty for this crime. Today, as we approach the new millennium, **the word is no longer treason but privatisation** and the penalty has been struck from our law books.

Jigsaw piece 2 - Another New Zealand politician was R......r D......s from whose Christian name was coined the word to cover all this restructuring i.e. Rogernomics. A report in the Christchurch 'Press', 26ᵗʰ September 1987, told us that *"Mr D......s has said that he is happy to sell the rest of the Government's shareholding, not just a further part of it, "next week", if he gets the right price."* (See also page 46 in our other book "Final Notice".)

The men in these two articles both belonged to the same political party

Now to throw the proverbial spanner in the works.

Jigsaw piece 3 - Here is a quote from the ex-Prime Minister of New Zealand, taken from the New Zealand 'Sunday Star', 27ᵗʰ January 1987. He spoke to representatives from different countries at a meeting in Rome. Remember that **his party was in opposition** to the aforementioned's party, **but look - he is speaking the same thoughts.**

"...to see what we could do to mobilise public opinion in our various

spheres of influence to give political support to the difficult decisions that have to be taken by the governments of the G7 to implement the policies that are seen to be necessary..

*....**The G7 proposal involves some loss of sovereignty by the participants...** "* (R......t M.......n). End quote. (See also page 245 of "Final Notice".)

Translation of this man's speech into simple English

"To you people reading this today, I must tell you of the plan **passed on to me by the G7**. We must try and sell this idea to the citizens of our many countries. This will not be easy, but obviously, we must listen to those who hold the financial purse strings. Great care must be exercised in not letting too much information out at one time lest the people become suspicious of our intentions and turn from us. You see, it is no longer a decision of choice for any political party of any persuasion. **It involves the selling out of the sovereignty of every nation on earth**, ultimately for the purpose of setting up a One World Government. With a careful use of language, the public can be conned into believing that this is ultimately a good move."

This now leads us in a natural progression on to -

Jigsaw piece 4 - The three men quoted earlier were merely **perpetrators** and not **designers** of this plan, therefore, do not be too harsh in your judgement of them. They simply did not possess the foresight to understand the end result of all their wheeling and dealing. If they had, they would have considered their children and grandchildren, whose lives will be drastically affected. (Please turn to page 243-245 in "Final Notice" for more notes on the G7's role.)

I've found it - I've found it - I've found it!

Another piece of the jigsaw has fallen into place. **Who is organising the world-wide, One World Government fiasco?** Once again, our ex-Prime Minister of New Zealand has been more than helpful.

The Adam Smith Institute

"I've never heard of it", I hear you cry. Don't be surprised. Neither have 99.9% of the earth's population which included, until fairly recently, this book's author.

'Waikato Times', 20th March 1996 - *"Reforms cited as example.*

The influential Adam Smith Institute has urged Britain to emulate New Zealand's public sector reforms in a report just released.

The think-tank named after the 18th century free market economist will also be addressed on the reforms by former Finance Minister, Sir R.....r D.......s at a meeting in Westminster on Friday.

....The Adam Smith Institute largely credits D....d L.....'s Labour Government for the changes which have led to New Zealand's balanced Budget, and faster economic growth, lower inflation and lower income tax rate than Britain." Break quote.

Author's note - **This article neglects to add the fact that most of New Zealand's assets are now controlled by overseas groups.**

Continue quote - *"They recommend that Britain should follow New Zealand's example and make the Bank of England independent with the governor made personally responsible for hitting a low inflation target.*

***In the last decade, New Zealand has been the world's laboratory for public sector reform"**, the authors say.*

*"If our politicians - from whichever party - want to know how to change Britain for good, they need merely to **book a flight to Auckland**."* End quote.

Who Are These Disruptive Characters?

1. The Adam Smith Institute was founded in 1977.
2. Its aim is to promote market-based economic reform internationally.
3. Its staff advise government leaders in five continents.
4. It is the only such organisation in the world.
5. It is named after Adam Smith (1723-1790) who believed in free markets, fair competition and limited government.
6. In the U.K. it has played a crucial role in privatisation.
7. It advises the U.K. Prime Minister.
8. It promotes government services to be "**contracted out**" e.g. New Zealand Telecom, May 1998.
9. It promotes reforming the welfare state - See New Zealand Budget 1998.
10. Its by-line is "**Making Ideas Change the World**".
11. It commenced its work in Great Britain and then moved world-wide.
12. Its clever psychology involves **"Public Choice Theory",** which gives the electorate the illusion that they have some say in the changes that are being made e.g. 'Samoa News', 21st April 1998 - **"How we feel about layoffs" and "How we feel about poker machines".**

Let us be perfectly frank about this. **The designers of the New World Order couldn't care less about what anyone thinks about anything**. Their plans are already set in concrete.

So much then for **referendums** and **public choice**. Giving all this advice to governments is certainly a very profitable business to be engaged in, however. Even the Kiwi entrepreneurs are into it now.

New Zealand 'Herald', 6th August 1997 - *"New Zealand Reform Consultants Earn $14 million.*

*New Zealand consultants selling advice on economic reforms earned $US9 million ($NZ14 million) from the World Bank in 1996, up from $4 million three years ago, Tradenz said. New Zealand consultants were able to show off their expertise on a mission to Washington where a briefing on New Zealand privatisation reforms was held with World Bank officials. **About 50 New Zealanders work at the World Bank.**"* End quote.

Author's note - Suggested seminar title - "How to sell your country and get paid for it!"

13. The ASI pioneered many of the techniques used in privatisation and stressed the importance of **involving** various interest groups including employees and customers.
14. They advised the introduction of private firms to do the **"contract out"** work for ex-government departments.
15. Make **schools and hospitals** independent of government interference.

During the months of May/June 1998, the New Zealand Fire Service was under attack - Sack the lot and let some reapply under a binding personal contract.

In simple English, the New World Order plan involves the government of each country surreptitiously, cunningly, and **gradually sliding out from all financial or funding responsibilities** e.g. 'Tomorrow's Schools' in New Zealand and 'Leading Schools' in Australia. What cute names for a massive con job that ultimately means the deprivation of a good, sound, education for our children. The whole education system has now been turned on its ear as both staff and parents spend much of their time in a desperate search for cash to keep the show on the road. A point to remember is that uneducated children however, will not challenge the New World Order. **Hello to bingo, raffles, and socials.**

Result - illiterate children who can't add up figures without a calculator, nor read the newspaper.

16. The ASI recommends huge reductions in bureaucratic committees (quangos) e.g. NZ, 1987.
17. Deregulation of industry, which in many cases destroys local industry as they cannot compete with cheaper imports.

18. The ASI pushes **speedy** market reform programmes. Using Fabian Socialistic ideas **speed is essential**. Masses of training seminars and conferences are essential. When asked to slow down the reforms, the ministers of finance refuse to do so. They can't because they are trapped by the secret plan.

19. Each country is specifically targeted e.g. Mongolia Privatisation Plan. Current situation, key issues, objectives, priorities, plans for bankrupt firms, regulatory reform and skills development.

Can you imagine privatising Mongolia? Video clips of that country normally reveal only horsemen playing games and conducting contests of skill and strength in the desert. **Maybe they are privatising saddles and bridles.**

20. **The ASI is now on the Internet - see http://www.adamsmith.org.uk** Please look this up and startle your friends.

21. They intend to replace Britain's welfare state by a **fully funded system**. Using the two examples of Singapore and Chile, both countries require their citizens to save for their own future retirement.

22. **They recommend the book entitled "The Kiwi Effect", sub-titled "What Britain Can Learn from New Zealand".**

The idea is presented that New Zealand is now far better off as a result of the 'slash and burn' policies on government programmes. Here they go again - lies, lies, and still more lies. I have yet to meet the New Zealander who feels our country is in better shape now than in pre-1987 when the so-called reforms commenced. It is actually quite horrible to observe the cost in **wreckage** of peoples' lives and in too many cases - **suicide**.

23. Henry Kissinger is credited with the statement, *"By controlling energy, we can control nations. By controlling food, we can control individuals."*

24. The ASI published a book entitled - "A Power of Good - The Verdict on Electricity Privatisation". City dwellers in Auckland, New Zealand, will give different advice if you ask them what happened when **their privatised power system collapsed early 1998.**

While this is happening, however, the ASI looks at **gains in efficiency and profitability**. Unfortunately, the Auckland privatisation scheme will prove to be worse than a damp squib if they still continue to use it as a success story.

25. **The ASI theme of the year was - Welfare Reform**. This is why New Zealand's latest Prime Minister, is busy at this time of writing, promoting

welfare cuts under the misnomer **"The Code for Moral and Social Responsibility. Poor Mr Howard in Australia is also trying so hard,** but the ASI policies are so ridiculous, it makes one very unpopular in the eyes of the electorate. I feel sorry for Prime Ministers and Ministers of Finance in every country that is forced to follow the Adam Smith Institute restructuring plans, as it leads to political suicide. Citizens of these countries should not be surprised to watch their leaders **receive the order of the boot** e.g. **Suharto and Hashimoto.**

Is all this making sense yet or have I taken on too big a task to convince you, the reader? This is a world-wide confidence job! It is also a gigantic conspiracy! You're still not convinced? Then let us carry on with more proof!

26. **The ASI now wants to privatise and sell up Britain's forests.** The catch-cry (and there must be some obscure phrase to cover each scam) is **"Forests for the People"**.

Since the majority of forests are in Scotland, it would represent a real transfer of ownership rights from a remote bureaucracy direct to the Scottish people. They forgot to mention that from there, ownership would quickly go overseas.

27. The ASI hosted Sir R......r D.........s, the principal architect of 'Rogernomics' at a House of Commons lecture in late March 1998. He devoted much of his address to the welfare system in New Zealand, and the urgency of moving to a funded system. So we see, he has left the New Zealand parliament and now addresses a group who formulate the policies for the parliament. **He therefore now wields more power than he did before.**

28. The ASI launched a programme for entrants to submit ideas on **how to save public funds**. You see, here it is again. Get everybody involved in the scheme until psychologically, they feel part of it. What a clever ruse!

29. The ASI met at St James Hotel for a lunch-time seminar on **Welfare State Reform**. An audience of 20 heard the 4 speakers. Notice only 20 were present. **Like the IMF, a small intelligent group can very easily manipulate the masses**.

30. The ASI met in April 1998 under the title "The Next Generation". The speaker spoke of trials and tribulations of advising foreign governments on market reform and privatisation and **strongly recommended avoiding the fermented yak's milk** offered by Mongolian hospitality.

31. NHS or the National Health Service comes under the umbrella of this group as they devise ways and means to **gradually** ease the government out from funding national health.

32. **Subsidies for farmers must be removed** said the British Prime Minister.

33. The ASI also **brings the environment** into their discussions. In politics, if you wish to remain credible, make sure the greenies like you.

34. Adam Smith, the founder of the concepts here discussed, would agree that it is cheaper to import than to subsidise local produce. The rationale presented is that fraud is stopped in its tracks as farmers no longer get paid for non-existent produce.

The Adam Smith Institute Guides Great Britain's Labour Government

35. The ASI rated their performance over the first 200 days. **They were given a two out of three.** The ASI's publication "New Labour's 200 Days - A hundred ideas in action."

    This of course shows us all how a Prime Minister is now regarded by this group. Simply
    - a **puppet**.

36. Subjects included
    a) Welfare to Work - just like New Zealand.
    b) Great Britain's Railway Privatisation
    c) The future privatisation of the London Underground. This latter reform has the stunning title of "Modernising London Underground Through Public-Private Partnerships."

37. Next to come in Great Britain is **road pricing** - just like New Zealand.

38. Later on the ASI suggests log books for houses and property.

39. The Fabian Society also is not excluded from their deliberations. Their forte is **"To conquer by stealth and gradualism"**.

That's Not All!

Another little-known think tank with similar ideas which many of us would label **subversive** is the – **Mont Pelerin Society.**

Founded 50 years ago by F.A. Hayek, it is dedicated to propagating the principles of a **free society and a free economy**. **This group has links to the guinea pig laboratory country of New Zealand** through a group called **The Business Round Table.** Some of this group's members also belong to the Mont Pelerin Society.

Until he died, F.A. Hayek was chairman of the Adam Smith Institute

panel of scholars. Here is the common denominator, **Hayek was involved in both groups.**

This group, in turn, has a massive financial ,and therefore psychological, grip on the government of New Zealand. **Simply put, if the politicians in power wish to retain their positions, they mustn't argue with the boss.** Therefore, in spite of the governments of the day continuously selling up our national assets and continuously churning out strange bills with odd-sounding titles, do not ever write them off as **mad-men and mad-women.**

In actuality, they are merely **trapped men and trapped women**.

Thus, some of George Bush's "1000 Points of Light", are gradually being revealed. We know of many others, but here is a short list. The jigsaw is coming together.

Pecking Order

- Lucifer
- Adepts - Elect - Sages in top level of Freemasonry
- Council on Foreign Relations
- The Bilderbergers
- The Tri-lateral Commission
- The Club of Rome
- The Bank for International Settlements
- The G8
- The International Monetary Fund
- The World Bank
- The Adam Smith Institute
- The Mont Pelerin Society
- The Business Round Table
- The Government of your country
- The poor ignorant people

The web site for the Mont Pelerin Society is http://www.cis.org.au/Policy/mps.html - it should give you a lot of food for thought.

Think Tanks

What are these? One might imagine a group of scholars seated in a large galvanised iron water tank, their fingers pressed against their temples, no sound coming from their lips, but all sorts of thoughts rushing through their frenzied brains.

But one would be wrong! The Webster's New World Dictionary tells

42

us that they are ...**a group or centre organised to do intensive research and problem solving.**

Government personnel, you understand, don't have the time, and in some cases, even the ability, to think through problems! It is for this reason that most parliamentarians select a large group, or even groups of advisors.

In New Zealand we have the **Business Round Table** offering their advice to the government of the day. (See also our book "Final Notice", page 42.) Note that as the New World Order will be led by business people and not political people, this piece of information is of supreme importance. This is why government departments have now been changed into businesses.

The Bank for International Settlements (BIS)

This group began as a result of the Hague Agreement of 1930. Carroll Quigley, in his book, "Tragedy and Hope", writes in 1966 - *"The powers of financial capitalism had a far reaching aim, nothing less than to **create a world system of financial control in private hands able to dominate the political system of each country and the economy of the world as a whole.**

...There does exist, and has existed for a generation, an international...network...This network which we may identify as **the Round Table Groups**, has no aversion to co-operating with the Communists, or any other groups, and frequently does so..."* End quote.

Author's note - In New Zealand, the guinea-pig test case country for New World Order, the Business Round Table played a major part in guiding government policy. Remember please, the Adam Smith Institute and the Mont Pelerin Society's links with the Business Round Table.

This group's name pops up quite regularly in the media columns and therefore, we thank Mr Quigley for helping us in our understanding of the part these businessmen play.

Always bear in mind, it is not what you know but who you know.

Rule - known and respected by all politicians. **"If you want to win the vote, woo the wealthy businessman and don't take his "suggestions" lightly."**

New Zealand's Business Round Table
or **Mad Hatter's Tea Party**

In an article written for the 'National Business Review', 3rd October 1983, we read in part - *"What is probably the most powerful and influential group in New Zealand outside Cabinet and the Treasury has decided to go public.*

The **New Zealand Business Round Table**, a group of 17 of the country's largest businesses, had made its membership list and aims available to the National Business Review...**its industrial and political clout is immense**.

Less politely, but probably more accurately, the Round Table is also known in the capital as the **Auckland (industrial) mafia.**

. . . the Round Table "bends over backwards" not to be seen as a pressure group able to influence Government policy, "but I suspect that, if we have a viewpoint, it would be listened to without necessarily being followed" - Chairman R.....n T.....r). End quote.

And 15 years later....

'Waikato Times', 16th January 1998 - *"Calls for the wholesale privatisation of local authority assets by **the Business Round Table** were simplistic, local government New Zealand President.......says.*

*Business Round Table executive director......last week said that New Zealanders would suffer economically and environmentally while water supplies stayed in local authority hands, as the confusion of political and commercial objectives meant **efficiency** was likely to suffer."* End quote.

Author's note - That I find is a very odd statement. This person, who apparently feels he has the right, without even being elected to government, to say what should happen to our water supplies is simply out of order. **Could this man also have links with the Mont Pelerin Society?** If so, we could well see some more of his way-out ideas in print.

Why did the news media even print his ridiculous ideas? New Zealand has been running its own water systems for over 150 years, and this man apparently considers us all to be fools. Any observer of the results of privatisation of a national asset, and subsequent selling overseas is simply saying, **"Please raise the costs for this service would you? Oh, thank you. We so enjoy paying more for everything!"**

The Cook Strait ferries, running between the two islands of New Zealand are owned by the Americans. Let us be perfectly frank here. The new American owners live 13-14 hours away from here by air. They obviously don't care a straw about us, as they increase the fares regularly, and make it a mammoth economic hurdle for the average New Zealand family to go on holiday over to the other island.

Business Round Table people don't know this of course because they always travel by air.

Back to the Hamilton Water Supply Again

Hamilton 'Press', 14th January 1998 - *"Hamilton City Council water, drainage and refuse manager.......said...."They are just testing the water, and fair enough for them....*

*It's business and they see New Zealand as a potential market." Mr....said he was **opposed to the privatisation of the water supply**.*

*He believed it would lead to **a substantial increase in the cost of water to Hamilton consumers.***

"It is literally a license to print money", he said." End quote.

There you go, Mr.....You and your Business Round Table friends go and have another exciting chat around your table and keep your foolish ideas to yourselves.

Christchurch 'Press', 3ʳᵈ January 1998 - *"Globalisation working well for New Zealand.*

Many see globalisation washing inexorably over national borders, beyond the ability of governments to control.

They say it is destroying the sovereignty of nations with unelected multinationals in the driving seat. There is also the belief that New Zealand has gone further down this road than other similar countries, that it has been reckless in its willingness to open its doors to the world...

....executive director of the New Zealand Business round Table, looks at the history of the country's economy..." End quote.

New Zealand 'Herald' headline - *"Globalisation can make **"us"** more secure and wealthier."* **When you read the word 'us', remember it is identifying members of the Business Round Table**.

Of course there are still 996 jigsaw pieces to go. These groups are all building a small part of the puzzle but believe me, there is a master planner or puppeteer who hopes to bring the whole thing together by the year 2000. This is why George Bush referred to the plan as New World Order but Jimmy Carter before him called it 'Global 2000'.

Q. Can we identify this master puppeteer?

A. We can indeed. He is represented by the eye in the triangle on the reverse side of every U.S.$1 bill.

This eye in the triangle is also found adorning many church buildings in various parts of the world. Of all these buildings, one is the Church of the Nativity in Bethlehem, and the other, the Church of the Annunciation in Nazareth. I've personally viewed these two sites at least 15 times so please take note.

Not only that, the Grand Master of the Freemasons' lodge has this eye in the triangle as part of his jewellery.

I often ask myself "Why do men not investigate all these things before

ANNOUNCING THE BIRTH OF THE NEW WORLD ORDER (WITHOUT GOD), UNDER THE ALL-SEEING EYE OF SATAN, THE ANTI-CHRIST, 666

they become involved in these ventures?" I, as a result, have to use up my valuable time finding out things that others wish to keep hidden. It is almost like a foolish child's game, yet the outcome will prove to be very deadly.

Who then is represented by this eye in the triangle?

Our book, "Better Than Nostradamus", tells the whole story and completely unmasks this rascal.

CHAPTER TEN

THE I.M.F. WOLF

There are some folk who still struggle with the concept that the IMF is portrayed in this book as the big bad wolf. How else can I portray any large group with such clout that it can -

a) lend a nation money

b) destroy or control that nation through its **conditions**.

You see, when New Zealand borrowed from the IMF in 1961, and the government of the day signed the **conditions**, do you think they could look in to the future and see the end result? Of course not!

The politicians of those days loved their country. They were loyal to their country. Unhappily, the same does not apply today. Little did the old time politicians know that the **independence and sovereignty** of the country was on the line.

At the beginning of 1998 -

a. Who controls New Zealand's largest **newspaper** chain? - **An Irishman**.

b. Who controls the **buses** in Wellington, New Zealand's capital city? - Stagecoach buses from **Scotland**.

c. Who is buying up Auckland city's **Yellow Bus Co?** - Stagecoach buses from **Scotland.** Interestingly enough, they also control the biggest bus company in Nairobi, Kenya. We see these buses regularly during our African visits.

d. Who controls the New Zealand **Railways?** - The **U.S.A.**

e. Who has had control of the most important service in New Zealand's restructured society i.e. **telecommunications**? - Ameritech - U.S.A. and Bell Atlantic - **U.S.A.**

And now that Ameritech feel they can make more money in Europe, they are selling their 24.9% stake in Telecom on an instalment basis in the United States. Thus the Americans hold on to what used to be one of New Zealand's most important assets.

Proof - Proof - Proof

'Time' magazine, 8th December 1997 - *"....In the past two weeks, they arrived by commercial airliners - a bunch of innocuous number crunchers from the International Monetary Fund...*

Just a few weeks before they arrived, Seoul had been calling the idea of an I.M.F. rescue **unthinkable***.*

...With Thailand and Indonesia receiving I.M.F. bailouts, the fund has become the main hope for containing the East Asian upheavals before they spread to Japan and from there, perhaps to the U.S." Break quote.

Author's note - Japan loves investing in other countries but to this point in history will not allow any country to invest in theirs. Notice how this clever plan will force them to reverse their policies.

Continue quote - *"...for all the embarrassment that attaches to it, a bid to the I.M.F. allows recipient governments to* **claim that an outside force is compelling them to make unpopular but necessary reforms***.*

...The organisation with all this power was established at the Bretton Woods conference near the end of World War II. **The goal was to build a new international economic order** *and thus avoid a repetition of the prewar period's spreading economic chaos* **which had set the stage for Hitler***." .*

Author's note - Believe me, the economic chaos we are now beholding is setting the stage for Antichrist. Hitler's behaviour was that of a Sunday School boy compared to this guy.

"And now ye know what withholdeth that he might be revealed in his time.

For the mystery of iniquity doth already work: only he who now letteth will let, until he be taken out of the way."[1]

South East Asia ready for the high jump.

What's going on? The tail end of 1997 has brought us strange news indeed. As one commentator put it - *"The Asian Tiger economies have tumbled one after another. Within days of the* **Thai** *collapse in July,* **Indonesia** *was afflicted by a run on its currency. That was followed by the collapse of the stock and currency markets in the* **Philippines** *and* **Malaysia***.*

The crash of the **Hong Kong** *stock-market last month sent stock-markets everywhere into a tail spin. Before share prices recovered, a run on the* **South Korean** *won threatened the world's 11th largest trading nation with bankruptcy."* End quote.

Let us outline them once more:

a. Thailand
b. Indonesia
c. Philippines
d. Malaysia
e. Hong Kong
f. South Korea

By accident? Certainly not!

The planners have already set up the western nations and at this quite late date, are now moving in on our eastern friends. The nations listed above, have to this point in history, remained quite strong and independent, economically speaking.

Kicking and Screaming

Thus a situation needed to be arranged so that they could be led kicking and screaming into the **IMF loans - conditions - reforms - privatising - sell out sovereignty, trap**. I guess it could be said of these people that they are possibly more business-wise than many of their western brethren. There are some folk in the guinea-pig nation of New Zealand who really think we are now better off, having sold out our sovereignty.

Big Bad Wolf

Now, who do you think is waiting in the wings with **loans and conditions** at the ready. You've got it - the IMF and friends! Before we continue with this explanation, let us list a few catchwords that seem to be used worldwide. Could it be the same groups who swung the wrecker's ball at the guinea-pig country of New Zealand, are now swinging the same wrecker's ball against South East Asia. This would appear to be the case.

Catch-Words

a. **Belt tightening** to be done
b. Economic reforms
c. **Pain** to be endured
d. Light at the end of the tunnel
e. **Level playing field**
f. Restructuring
g. Layoffs
h. Downsizing
i. Bank for International Settlements (BIS)
j. International Monetary Fund (IMF)
k. World Bank
l. Redundancies
m. Retrenchment
n. Structural Readjustment
o. Confidence
p. Freemarket reforms

A brief look at Thailand

The 'Herald', 9th December 1997 - *"Thailand closes finance doors to rebuild system.*

Overseeing....is a government appointed **Financial Restructuring Agency...**

In Washington yesterday an International Monetary fund (IMF) executive board met....for Thailand.

...But in the short term, the moves are set to be **painful**. **"There will be a lot of pain** in the short term..."

...The reality hit hard at firms ordered to close with many employees collapsing in tears after the decision to close 56 firms was made public.

"Many of my friends here are crying. Not only have we lost our jobs, but a lot of us here have heavy debts, like house payments," said an *employee....*" End quote.

Many nations were involved in the bail out of Thailand even Australia and little New Zealand. Why did we agree to help? We had no choice - **IMF conditions** you understand.

Korea in the 'Kaktus'

'Sunday Star Times', 2nd December 1997 - *"Korean loan brings IMF new pressure.*

A $95.84 billion bailout for troubled South Korea will bite deep into the resources of the International Monetary Fund, and new crises could force the fund itself to beg for cash, say officials." End quote.

Q. Why would the IMF risk going into debt over one country's economic problems?

A. They have to, as Korea is the lever being used to open all the **other South East Asian closed oyster economies.**

'Herald', 22nd November 1997 - *"Over time, Korea may need as much as $100 billion, a bailout that would rank among the largest since the second world war, economists said....**a full scale collapse would reverberate around the world...**"* End quote.

What is the cause of the problem?

Although we have already seen the true cause was evil manipulation, **the official reason given for the meltdown lies in excess production**. No doubt, this was woven into the crash cause as well. (See pages 9 & 10 in our third book 'Final Notice', printed in 1989.)

These countries in South East Asia must keep producing or they go under. Now, the moment of truth has arrived. They are going under!!!

The problem with the IMF

'Herald', 24th November 1997 - *"The IMF is an oxygen mask for the Korean economy, which cannot breathe on its own,"* said an editorial in the Joong-Ang Ilbo newspaper. *"Our pride is gone now that the **economic model student of developing nations** (Korea) has sought an IMF bailout package."* Break quote.

Author's note - please remember that New Zealand was the model student of the Western nations. That country is still in bondage to the loans, conditions and selling up of sovereignty scam.

"...I'm terribly disappointed that we asked for IMF aid," said An Seung II, an accountant in Seoul. *"Now we have to **tighten our belts** to fix the problems, the **pains** we'll have will be much bigger than the ones we have now..."* End quote.

This means that this man is clearly a reader of international newspapers. He knows the **catchwords** and also that the Korean economic problems will be minor in the light of the destructive reforms the IMF is going to impose on his country.

Goodbye Korea

'Herald', 2nd December 1997 - *"South Korea haggled with the International Monetary Fund over **policy demands attached to a massive financial bailout plan** fearing this could topple thousands of companies and double unemployment...*

"Until you have the last 't' crossed and the last 'i' dotted, the agreement is not there," said IMF managing-director, Michel Camdessus...

*"If they don't put the finger on the pulse of what really brought the economy down, it is harder to see them going through with the **economic restructuring** that is needed down the line,"* said ......research director at Coryo Research Institute..."* Break quote.

Note here that this poor man clearly doesn't understand what is really going on here. He obviously thinks that the cause of the problem lies within his own country.

Continue quote - *"**Union's vow to take action if jobs are threatened**..."* Break quote.

Another fruitless line of irrelevant jargon, as under the One World Government, collective bargaining and unions become obsolete. **Every would-be worker** will sign a **personal contract.**

Continue quote - *"...The main sticking point, local media reports say, is whether to shut down as many as 12 of 30 finance companies, known in*

*Korea as merchant banks. Those which fail to meet capital standards set by the **Bank for International Settlements** may be forced to close..."* End quote.

On pages 3-4 of our book "Second Warning", written in 1984, please read again and observe what was written: *"...a man leaning against the glass door of a bank. He has a very sad look in his eyes - reason - above his head is written one word only - **CLOSED....**"* End quote.

And now, ladies and gentlemen, for your further interest, we turn to our newspaper once more in the month of December 1997 and read: *"**Korean crisis deepens as more banks close**.*

'Dominion', 1ˢᵗ January 1998 - *"Fresh IMF support eases threat of South Korean default.*

South Korea limped into the new year amid indications that its looming debt catastrophe may have been averted for now thanks to fresh support from the International Monetary Fund and international bankers....

*...**In exchange for the aid, South Korea has flung open its financial markets, lifting almost all restrictions on foreign investment in the stock and bond markets**, allowing the won currency to float and significantly ease capital controls..."* End quote.

I sat looking at the incomplete puzzle and wondered why we, in little New Zealand, need to show any interest in the economic collapse of Korea, or any other country for that matter.

We're all locked in together!

Remember the movie entitled, **"No man's an Island?"** I hate to admit it but the whole plan is so clever no-one but the devil himself could have devised it. The key to the whole scenario is **trade**.

The 'Nelson Mail', 31ˢᵗ December 1997 - *"South Korea's crippled economy has forced Nelson fishing companies to seek other buyers for their **sea-food**.*

...Korea has shut down, they are importing just the bare essentials...

South Korea's problems have also caused concern for the forestry industry in Nelson." End quote.

Not only **fishing** and **forestry** have been affected but **tourism** has declined to such a degree, Korean Airlines barely fly to our shores any more and fourthly, **students** are not coming either.

No matter which country you belong to, these cunning rascals have been secretly working overtime to make sure the rule sticks. *"If one suffers, we all suffer!"*

A prophecy in obscure language dated about 51 AD draws our attention at this point.

"For the mystery of iniquity doth already work only he who now letteth will let, until he be taken out of the way."[2]

<u>Interpretation</u> - At a certain time in history a very evil plan will envelope the world. This plan will subject every citizen of the world to a life of obedience to a man titled Antichrist. He will control a One World Government.

Things are certainly moving along at a pace.

What about North Korea?

'Herald', 12th December 1997 - *"Communism on its knees in North Korea.*

...here is a state on its knees. Both industrial and agricultural production on the edge of oblivion...

*Its nuclear industry that had Western strategists screwing themselves into contortions to prove that it was able to produce bombs and missiles that would wreak havoc far and wide, is in reality, in the infant stage. Incredible though it now seems, it is only three years ago that the United States, frightened out of its mind by this **crumbling pygmy** went to the brink of war..."* End quote.

Never forget please that all communistic regimes must shortly collapse, as must all capitalistic systems world-wide.

Why is this?

The New World Order or one world government system is to be controlled by big business ruling a restructured world, controlled by a synthesis of communism and capitalism.

Therefore, prepare for both China and Cuba to shortly change their systems.

I repeat, it is for this reason that all governments of the world are **surreptitiously pulling out of funding their ex-government departments** and handing over control of these to private business interests e.g. In New Zealand in 1998, hospitals, police departments and fire departments were all in an uproar. You see, without this information, the actions of the government just don't make sense. No wonder the people are baffled. **It's those jolly 'think tanks' again!**

A Public Challenge

Some bold person, with some prestige in society, needs to publicize the role of the Adam Smith Institute and the Mont Pelerin Society in New Zealand politics.

The public would be outraged if only they knew. Particularly the policemen and the firemen who are absolutely baffled as to why they are being indiscriminately laid off.

War Ahead?

There is still talk of a North Korean invasion of South Korea, as at this time of writing, the Northerners are in desperate straits.

The Hegelian Dialectic, which acts as the basis for all world government plans, reads thus - **"From this system of Hegelian philosophy, comes the historical dialectic i.e. that all historical events emerge from a conflict between opposing forces."**

The Berlin Wall

The collapse of this unnatural barrier between East and West Germany was the beginning of the end for communism. We predicted this collapse in our public meetings well before it took place. How was this? We already understood that little piece of the jigsaw. Page 96, no.2, in our first book 'Warning' says clearly that *"Communism will link up with and be absorbed by this E.E.C. monster..."*

Thus it is becoming clear, I trust, that as the pieces of the jigsaw come together, a very clear plan emerges -

i.   Communism is finished.
ii. Capitalism is being rapidly destroyed.
iii. The IMF is playing a major role in this plan.

Their task is so simple in this economic climate. **Reorganise debt proposals so that national sovereignty is eliminated.**

A Big Satan

'EIR', 23rd September 1988 - *"The overall approach was laid out by IMF Director-General, Michel Camdessus, in a recent interview to a German newspaper.*

"If a country thinks the IMF is big satan, or a criminal organisation, we can't do anything for such a country naturally. We only work with those countries that want to work with us." End quote.

If the economic plan fails, **the food weapon** can then be used. Flood and famine wrecked Sudan which was isolated from the international financial community. They refused IMF interference with their loans and conditions, resulting in a loss of sovereignty and now, genocide.

Disclaimer - To avoid workers in the IMF system getting excited and thoughts of litigation cropping up in their minds, we hasten at this stage to assure such persons that this chapter is in no way meant as a personal attack on their characters or credibility. They are, in the main, simply working within a framework which has been prepared for them. The vast majority are good industrious people. Only those with the ability to see the wider picture of this jigsaw puzzle can see the end result i.e. a **One World Government**!

FOOTNOTES

[1]   II Thessalonians 2:6-7

[2]   II Thessalonians 2:6-7

CHAPTER ELEVEN

CORRUPT UNLIMITED POWER (THE INTERNATIONAL MONETARY FUND)

New Zealand 'Herald', 12th January 1998 - *"About 30 per cent of Thai youngsters under the age of 15 believe the International Monetary Fund (IMF) is an unidentified flying object (UFO). The IMF came to rescue the Thai economy in August but a survey of 1648 children showed that only a quarter of them knew what it was and many believed it to be an object from outer space."* End quote.

'Time' magazine, 8th December 1997. In an article entitled *"IMF, the Rescue"*, the author, strangely enough seems to be agreeing with the writer of this book. *"Just a few weeks before they arrived, Seoul had been calling the idea of an IMF rescue unthinkable.*

...With Thailand and Indonesia receiving IMF bailouts, the fund has become the main hope for containing the East Asian upheavals, before they spread to Japan and from there, perhaps to the U.S.

...For all the embarrassment that attaches to it, a bid to the IMF allows recipient governments to claim that an outside force is compelling them to make unpopular but necessary reforms.

...The organisation with all this power was established at the Bretton Woods conference near the end of World War II. The goal was to build a new international economic order...

...The organisation today operates from a headquarters in Washington, only a few blocks from the White House, which alone makes it suspect in the eyes of some countries.

...The IMF staff is small, just 1,100 professionals, including 759 economists - only one fifth the size of its sister agency, the World Bank, which was established at the same time and funds development projects in the Third World.

IMF staff members constantly roam the globe, visiting countries and meeting with finances ministers and central bank governors." Break quote.

Author's note - Now you know why the finance minister in your particular country brings out such unusual budgets. They must simply **obey the conditions**, if their country has previously accepted the **IMF loans**.

Continue quote - *"Because the IMF releases its funds in periodic amounts, **it has a lever to keep countries in line**.*

*...The organisation itself has operated with a high level of **secrecy**, if not **mystery**, that has inflamed critics.*

*...Even when they work, the **remedies** the fund imposes as the price for handing out credit or money can be **nasty, brutish and not so temporary**. The Philippines has been under IMF supervision for three decades. Following IMF admonitions, the country **has enjoyed considerable success** in the past five years.*

1. Dismantling government monopolies.

2. Selling off state enterprises.

3. Opening its banking and telecommunications system." Break quote.

Author's note - Please read 2 or 3 times, the following statement.

Continue quote - *"Applying to the fund means **lost economic sovereignty** which is no small matter.*

*...The fund's recommendations also mean **pain** for the poor and working classes...higher taxes and lower social spending an **end to subsidies** on things like food and fuel and **privatisation** of inefficient state-owned industries, with the inevitable worker layoffs.*

...In Thailand, the IMF plan required the government to close 58 financial institutions.

*...**Rather than restoring confidence, the IMF's intervention merely confirmed to investors that they were right to flee**."* End quote.

Strangely enough, almost every article I have read on the IMF is **critical** of its methods. This was not previously the case in 1961 when **they first loaned money to the guinea-pig country of New Zealand**. Of course, 36 years later, it is easy to make an informed and intelligent judgement on these matters.

Come with me on an **opinions search** in the years 1997/1998.

'Straits Times', 17th December 1997 - *"It is time for the world to take a serious look at the International Monetary Fund. **In the past three months, this small, secretive institution has dictated economic conditions to 350 million people** in Indonesia, South Korea, the Philippines and Thailand.*

...Yet the IMF decisions have been taken without any public debate, comment or scrutiny.

*...**Staff at the fund...are unaccountable**.*

*...**The situation is out of hand**. However useful the IMF may be to the world community, **it defies logic to believe that the small group of 1,000 economists on 19th Street in Washington should dictate the economic***

ANNOUNCING THE BIRTH OF THE NEW WORLD ORDER (WITHOUT GOD), UNDER THE ALL-SEEING EYE OF SATAN, THE ANTI-CHRIST, 666

conditions of life to 75 developing countries with around 1.4 billion people.

*These people constitute 57 per cent of the developing world outside **China and India which are not under IMF programmes**."* Break quote.

Author's note - **They will be soon enough!** Please watch the news media closely during the year 1998. Again, I reiterate, the following countries must be brought down very soon and be put under **the IMF loans and conditions plan** resulting finally in **loss of sovereignty**. **Singapore, China, Hong Kong, India, and Taiwan**. (Date of writing - 23rd January 1998.)

Continue quote - *"The IMF threw together a draconian programme for Korea in just a few days, without deep knowledge of the country's financial system, and without any subtlety as to how to approach the problems.*

***Consider what it said about Korea just three months ago** in its 1997 annual report.*

"Directors welcomed Korea's continued impressive macro-economic performance, and praised the authorities for their enviable fiscal record"...

In the same report, the IMF had this to say about Thailand, at that moment on the edge of the financial abyss.

"Directors strongly praised Thailand's remarkable economic performance and the authorities' consistent record of sound macro-economic policies."

*...**There is no "fundamental" reason for Asia's financial calamity except financial panic itself.***

... Months ago, when the financial crisis began, the fund could have quietly encouraged Japan, the U.S. and Europe to provide some credit support to the Bank of Korea.

*...**With appropriate confidence building measures**, Korea could probably have got by with a modest slow-down in growth, no credit crunch, and a realistic time horizon of a few years to complete its needed financial reforms.*

*In more than six dozen developing countries, **the IMF is in a position to choose make or break policies**. While its instincts are often correct, they can sometimes be wrong with serious consequences.*

...Three general conclusions can be reached. First, the IMF is vested with too much power...

Second, the IMF's executive board should do its job of overseeing the staff. It is high time the board consulted outside expertise...

Third, IMF operations should be made public." End quote.

Author's note - Although the writer of this article is the head of the Harvard Institute for International Development, and contributed this article to the 'Financial Times', it is clear that he is not aware of the **conspiratorial** nature of the IMF activities. His three main concluding points appear to lack nothing, yet the IMF have to obey their superiors, the BIS (Bank for International Settlements), who in turn follow their leader's rules.

Now, I think you will enjoy this enlightened criticism of the IMF. 'International Herald Tribune', 6th January 1998 - *"The International Monetary Fund and the U.S. government are both playing with fire. The Asian financial crisis is the **most serious threat to global prosperity** since the oil shock of 1973.*

*The IMF was designed in 1944 expressly to prevent the currency deflations and exported financial panics that deepened the **Great Depression**. It was intended to anchor monetary stability, contain panics, discourage currency speculation and allow countries to grow their way out of recessions. But the IMF is now the premier instrument of deflation, as well as **the most unaccountable institution in the world**.*

*When a country gets into financial difficulty, it does what the IMF says - or goes into default and faces worse calamity. Of course, the IMF works hand in glove with the U.S. government, **so its victims** are correct to see it as a surrogate for U.S. power.*

The IMF has a one-size-fits-all economic programme to impose in any crisis.

***Tighten your belts and open your markets.** In return, it offers financial aid..."* End quote.

Author's note - All these media persons have suddenly become critics of IMF policies. But sadly it is **too late!**

New Zealand 'Herald', 12th January 1998 - *"Harvard economist....has blamed the International Monetary Fund for **aggravating** Asia's financial crisis, but says regional economies should recover before long.*

... "My sense is that the IMF added to the panic", he said, saying that the fund had erred by using the same rescue techniques employed in the past, instead of specific remedies tailored to the differing needs of Asian economies.

"The IMF took its normal remedy off the shelf and started to apply it", he said. He criticised the IMF's demand for bank closures in Indonesia, Thailand and South Korea, which was part of its bailout package.

The move sent the wrong signals to the market, Mr....said...."Private foreign investors had followed their peers in jumping out of the Asian markets without fundamental justification", he said." End quote.

Even the World Bank is Upset with the IMF

'Daily Telegraph', 9th January 1998 - *"The World Bank and its sister institution, the International Monetary Fund, are believed to be at odds over how to tackle the Asian economic and financial crisis.*

The IMF, which is leading a $57 billion rescue package for South Korea, has prescribed major changes and austerity measures to the troubled Asian economies.

But....chief economist at the World Bank and formerly President Clinton's senior economic advisor said, **"These are crises in confidence. You don't want to push these countries into severe recession".**

...One ought to focus on things that caused the crisis, not on things that make it too difficult to deal with.

...The IMF's measures are also generating criticism among Wall St analysts who fear they may provoke an ever deeper crisis." End quote.

Author's note - Deeper crisis indeed! They ain't seen nothin' yet. Wait until the IMF gets its claws into Singapore, India, China and Taiwan. That leads naturally on to Japan, then the U.S., then **goodbye world economy**.

The Trade Unions Pipe Up

I personally think it is imperative that they do try to fight back. I mean to say, what have they got to lose. They are completely ignorant as to all this information, so have a go, boys! At this time of writing, trade unions worldwide are **singing their swan-song**. They have served their purpose up until this point in history and acted out their aggressive part admirably. Following the world government's chief philosopher and his Hegelian Dialectic, this is how it was done.

Big Bosses and Big Business	- Thesis
Trade Union Power	- Antithesis
One World Government	- Synthesis

Please feel sad for the unionists in their death struggle.

'San Francisco Chronicle', 8th January 1998 - *"...In South Korea, austerity has a big enemy. The country's organised labor, unlike Thailand's tiny union sector or the pliant, government controlled unions in Mexico and Indonesia, is large and militant. Korean labor leaders threatened this week to resist layoffs or wage-cuts with "bloody" nation-wide strikes - a threat experts take seriously.*

...*The IMF's failure to stop the Asian decline has emboldened such liberal U.S. organisations as* **50 Years is Enough**, *a coalition of more than 200 groups that lobbies for the IMF and the World Bank to open their records and deliberations to public scrutiny and to pay more attention to how their policies affect the poor.*

"In Mexico and Asia, those countries' people will be paying for the bailouts for years to come", says..... an international finance analyst.....and a key member of 50 Years is Enough.

The **conditionalities** *(the key word - thank you) the IMF imposes* **merely reproduce the same abuses that brought on the crisis**.

...*The Clinton administration is expected to ask Congress to approve $18 billion for the IMF to boost its reserves. The IMF says, that if more crises occur - or if existing ones worsen, as now seems likely,* **it will simply run out of cash**.*"* End quote.

Korea 'Times', 13th January 1998 - *"Asian trade union leaders in the financial sector, have denounced the International Monetary Fund's (IMF) policy prescription for ailing countries in the region.*

At their worst, the IMF policies can be seen as an attempt to impose upon a country and a region, economic and social values which are inappropriate and threaten to undo decades of economic growth, social development, and ethnic cohesion...

FIET, based in Geneva, has about 11 million members from the private sector in more than 400 unions in 120 countries." End quote.

The IMF response to this is strictly - we don't care!

Mind Boggling Info

'West Australian', December 1987 - *"Japanese Prime Minister....Hashimoto, delivered the bluntest of messages to ASEAN this week:* **there is no Asian way out of this mess - it's the International Monetary Fund or nothing.**

...*This is the same Mr Hashimoto whose senior finance officials were hawking the concept of an "Asia fund" around the region only four months ago, as a* **sympathetic alternative to the IMF's foul-tasting medicine.**

...*"Reality is that* **aid is not possible without IMF conditionality."** End quote.

Author's note - Thank you, Mr Hashimoto. We are now all beginning to understand the true position. Be sure that if there was any other way out, South East Asian countries would take that way, rather than the IMF loans, conditions and sovereignty sell-out plan.

The People In South East Asia are Stunned!

Don't laugh. Your country could well be next on the agenda.

New Zealand 'Herald', 12th January 1998 - *"......chief economist of Singapore-based broking firm, J.M. Sassoon, best described the prevailing sentiment in Asia.* **"Everyone is still is a daze, too stunned to do anything, hoping this nightmare will go away".**

*Looking ahead, Asia is likely to spend this year picking up the wreckage **caused by international investors' rampant dumping of Asian assets.***

...Early optimism over some Asian countries' ability to recover has been dashed by a weaker than expected upturn in the electronics cycle. **Singapore, Taiwan and South Korea are key exporters of electronics components."** Break quote.

Author's note - It will be of interest to see which main product has been assigned to each of these South East Asian nations by the New World Order manipulators. The key word again - **Interdependence**.

Continue quote - *"The big unknown is whether China will also succumb **to the international investment community's punishment.***" Break quote.

Author's note - What an interesting turn of phrase.

Continue quote - *"China's got the same economic excesses. It's banking system has got little experience in risk management.* **China's fall would make what happened in South East Asia look like a party in comparison...**" End quote.

Author's note - China must fall and it must happen soon. (Date of prediction - 23rd January 1998.)

I trust that it is all becoming clear to you. The next question we must ask is, if the whole economic and social system of the world is being deliberately manipulated, and countries are being sold out, that is treason. Why not hang the perpetrators?

CHAPTER TWELVE

TREASON (PRIVATISATION) - HANG THEM ALL!

Imagine, a long wooden beam with many ropes, each fashioned in the form of a noose.

The padres are muttering and reading from their black books, as lines of men, all dressed in business suits, and joined to one another with ankle-shackles and chains, shuffle along, each to stand upon his own special trapdoor.

The hangman, dressed all in black, peers through the slits in his hood, awaiting the signal from his superior. Each of these men, the country's leading politicians who signed the IMF loans and conditionalities policies, along with those who specialised in the privatising and selling off of government assets, thereby committing treason, are asked if they have any last words.

By now, all the former arrogance and witty remarks seem to have become lost in the seriousness of the moment. One of them, the chief advocate for all this restructuring, his whole body shaking, his face white with fear and trepidation, glances around desperately as he tries to explain. "I felt I was so privileged to belong to so many secret world government groups. I would travel to New York, first class of course, at the tax-payer's expense. Nothing was spared, as I enjoyed the high life, the adoration, the bowing and scraping, the luxury.

I believed the words of advice from the big businessmen in my home country when they told me that all this would **improve efficiency**. I didn't really care about the poor folk who **committed suicide** through the implementation of my policies.

I believed the lies regarding global warming, the depletion of the ozone layer, and the disappearance of endangered species. I was sure that if we all worked together in a global village type of partnership, we would win.

Books about this subject were handed to me by enthusiastic members of my electorate but I only read a few lines and then scornfully referred to the authors as 'prophets of doom'. They had it all wrong whilst I had it all right.

But now, **it was my foolishness that brought about the loss of sovereignty and independence of my country**. My wife and children shout scorn at me. **Our freedoms that we enjoyed so much are all gone, never to be returned.**

My colleagues and I, in the flush of political enthusiasm signed and ratified all the U.N. treaties presented to us, not realising that they were all part of an organised plan to steal our independence.

The OECD plan which was also presented to us entitled MAI should have made us suspicious. Surely allowing some overseas investors the same rights as local investors to buy up the remaining assets of our country - I must have been crazy to have even considered such an outrageous lie!"

A murmur of assent from the crowd ripples through the marble-paved hall.

"Why was I so arrogant? Why wouldn't I listen to reason? What a terrible mess I have made. There is no longer anything left for my children to look forward to. It's all been sold. Gone forever into the hands of those deceitful, shadowy, lying, characters, pushing the One World Government concept.

Hangman - perform your duty. We are ready!"

Why Not?

In the test-case, guinea-pig country of New Zealand, the government of the day, in the main, unaware of what was about to take place, followed the suggestions of 5 conspirators, yet earlier on, passed a bill banning hanging as the penalty for treason.

Why?

They were about to embark on the IMF wrecking policies. Their motto - **"Better sure than sorry"!**

What About Great Britain?

Please recognise that Prime Minister, Tony Blair, is just beginning to follow the **conditionalities** that went along with Great Britain's **loans**. (May 1998)

Without becoming over-dramatic, let us watch Great Britain with interest and see if they also follow New Zealand and pass a quick bill cancelling hanging as being the penalty for treason. Otherwise, some clued up lawyer may take advantage of a very ancient law and arrange for a neck-tie party.

'Daily Telegraph', 3rd October 1997 - *"State's ultimate penalty will soon be just history.*

On July 10, 1992, Tony Teare was sentenced to death for the contract killing of Corinne Bentley, a care worker.

The judge, who did not don his black silk cap, was the Deemster of the Court of General Goal on the Isle of Man. Teare's sentence was commuted to life imprisonment in 1994 after the island became the final part of the United Kingdom to abolish hanging for murder.

The last executions on the mainland took place 30 years earlier.

...The pair died simultaneously in Strangeways Prison, Manchester, and Walton prisoner, Liverpool, on August 13, 1964.

...Methods of execution were refined to a single one - hanging. The last beheading was that of Lord Lovat in 1747. The last burning alive was in 1789.

...Between 1908 and 1927, 273 Britons were **hanged**, mostly for murder but some, like **Sir Roger Casement, the Irish statesman, for treason.** Between the wars, an average of 18 people a year were hanged.

...The abolition of capital punishment for murder means that in **England and Wales, a civilian can only be hanged for a few highly unusual offences.**

They are **treason** (technically, if the crown thinks fit, this crime can also be punishable by beheading), **the murder of a monarch,** and **certain offences against the Royal Family** and **piracy involving violence..**

...It is perhaps not surprising that Britain's last working gallows, in Wandsworth Prison, south London, was quietly dismantled four years ago... ". End quote.

CHAPTER THIRTEEN

SOUTH EAST ASIAN CRUNCH TIME (EARLY 1998)

Early January 1998, our office manager was asked by some television folk in Great Britain if it was possible to send me over to that country for one week. The reason for this was that I was to be involved in around 10 television interviews on these subjects. The estimated possible viewing audience, they told us, was 64 million.

I was informed that all other airlines were booked out but would Korean Airlines be okay as there were still seats available? Not only that, there was a substantial saving of more than $600 on the fares being offered. I chose Korean airlines without first looking at a world map to pinpoint its position.

Consequently, I left Auckland for London, via Nadi, Fiji, and Seoul, Korea, on the evening of the 6th January 1998.

Just north of Fiji, we passed through an area where three tropical cyclones were vying for position, which I found to be most interesting and uncomfortable. Later on in the night, I saw masses of lights down below on the right hand side of the plane. Upon asking the stewardess where we were, she replied, "That is Japan, sir!"

"Japan?" I spluttered, overcome with shock. "I thought I was on my way to London.

"Where is that world map again?" Too much travel, I guess, leads to **"familiarity breeds carelessness"**. Some readers may question my sanity in boarding a plane without realising exactly where it was going, however, it would all work out for the best.

We arrived in Seoul early the next morning and the temperature was -5 degrees Celsius with snow on the ground. Remember, I left New Zealand in the middle of summer. Five and a half hours later, we took off once more for London. I peered out the window all day looking at China, Siberia and Russia, and silently thanked the Lord that I was not born in that area of the world.

We flew into London over Europe which had just been experiencing vicious storms and after a week of television interviews, I returned home the same way.

Hot off the Press

Just before leaving my home for the Great Britain trip, I happened to read some words written by King Solomon in about the year 970 BC which certainly seemed very applicable to me that very day.

"A man's heart deviseth his way, but the Lord directeth his steps."[1]

This extra long journey was therefore not an accident! You will now be able to read information gleaned right from the trouble centre itself.

Important Initial Facts

During my 5½ hour stopover, I was able to converse with many businessmen and others. These folk were obviously all in a state of shock and were all asking the same question - "Who is to blame?"

I could then clearly understand that the whole scenario has been carefully planned to catch all the countries of Asia in the world government trap.

Hegelian Dialectic

The German philosopher named Hegel, is the one whose philosophies are being followed by the New World Order organisers.

1. **Create the problem.**
2. **Solve the problem.**

Catch Words

As your eye scans the following articles, please take careful note of the catch words and phrases. Many of these were used in New Zealand, the guinea pig test case country away back in 1987.

Proof 1 - The 'Korea Herald', 7th January 1998. *"President Kim Young-sam and President elect, Kim Dae-jung, yesterday, jointly urged Korea's large business conglomerates called (wait for it) "chaebols" to implement drastic self-reform measures.* (This is a Korean catchword.)

...The reforms should be carried out without any hesitation because there is not much time left, the President-elect said.

"I am confident that bright light will descend upon our economy (hey - he forgot the words - 'at the end of the tunnel' - the naughty boy.)

...Kim Dae-jung also called upon the people to further tighten their belts..." (Thank you Kim.) End quote.

Proof 2 - 'Korea Herald', 13th January 1998. *"...the National Assembly is to convene a special session Thursday to tackle the allowance of massive layoffs at Korean companies.*

...The current law in effect bars companies from firing unionised employees in masses for **downsizing purposes**.

...*Even visiting IMF director, Michel Camdessus plans to meet with **the nation's labour leaders** today to enlist their support in carrying out the labour reform...*" End quote.

Author's note - The laws will soon be changed in all these countries to **outlaw collective bargaining** and in it workers will all be obliged to sign **personal contracts**. Therefore, there will be no more threat of strikes.

Proof 3 - 'Evening Post', Wellington, 6 January 1998. *"The (IMF) Fund doles out loans to countries that are short of the U.S. dollars and other currencies they need to pay obligations to foreigners. In exchange the countries pledge to adopt **belt-tightening measures**, and take steps to **restructure their economies**...*" End quote.

The 'Korea Herald', 7th January 1998. *"Financial panic accompanying back-to-back corporate bankruptcies may hit in March as domestic banks have to meet the 8 per cent capital adequacy ratio requested by the **Bank for International Settlements (BIS)**...*" End quote.

Proof 4 - 'Korean Herald', 7th January 1998. *"With concerns mounting that the IMF imposed **bailout conditions** might touch off **massive layoffs**, the government plans to raise a job security fund of up to 4.5 trillion won to assist unemployed workers, a top government official said today.*

*...But the new government will set an example before asking workers and citizens to **"share the pain"** according to .....spokesman for Kim.*

*Kim also asked the Labour Minister to map out measures to **minimise redundancies** in the process of **structural readjustment** of businesses."* End quote.

Proof 5 - The New Zealand 'Herald', 24 November 1997. *"The IMF is an oxygen mask for the Korean economy which cannot breathe on its own...Our pride is gone, now that the economic model student of developing nations has sought **an IMF bailout package**.*

..."I'm terribly disappointed that we asked for IMF aid", said....an accountant in Seoul.

*Now, we have to **tighten our belts** to fix the problems, **the pains** will have to be much bigger than the ones we have now."* End quote.

Proof 6 - 'International Herald Tribune', 6th January 1998 - *"An age old Korean practice, common among housewives, draws together a group of* *acquaintances to pool their cash savings and trust one among them to manage the pool profitably. Often, that means providing the money to a credit-starved business at high interest rates. They also found that this allowed them to avoid reporting their holdings to South Korea's aggressive tax authorities.*

*...Financial methods and practises left over from a simpler era are abruptly clashing with the demands of a more modern society, like **accountability and openness**, and it is as true for big conglomerates as it is for housewives.*

*...By and large, Koreans did not seem surprised that a **system of bribery**, politically motivated laws and fiscal irresponsibility was widely practised by heads of conglomerates.*

*...An American author observed in his book about South Korea, "**The old order is shrivelling, but the new one has yet to be born.**"* End quote.

Author's note - This type of reporting is common when countries are undergoing IMF reforms. The message it sends out is clear. "**Look, South Korea was playing the economic fool, and they really needed us to help them come back into line - for their own good, of course! Later on they will be so grateful and will thank us for our help!**"

In the guinea pig country of New Zealand, the same scenario was played out as one of the political perpetrators of this diabolical restructuring wrote a book illustrating the slack economic habits of the New Zealand Railways, before he and his mates came riding in on their 'white horses' to 'rescue us'. **Oh, how grateful we are to know to know that our valuable railways asset is now in American hands.**

Korean Shortages

'Korean Herald', 13th January 1998 - *"Domestic manufacturers are caught up in a near-stalemate to secure imported raw materials due to the won's plunge against the greenback...*

The stockpiles of some raw materials, including oil, leather, natural rubber and textiles are expected to run out within a month, unless some measures are taken..." End quote.

All Countries Linked are in Trouble!

Now it becomes clear that each country affects its neighbour. 'Marlborough Express', 8th January 1998 - *"Export log trade in trouble.*

New Zealand's massive log export trade to South Korea may drop away 'significantly' in coming weeks and months, according to Fletcher Forests, one of the two big suppliers to that market.

Fletcher Forests said log exports worth tens of millions of dollars a year, were in doubt because of importer's problems with South Korea's banking system." End quote.

The New Zealand 'Herald', 22nd November 1997 also spoke of problems with beef, dairy products and kiwi-fruit exports.

Airlines Affected

'Press', 17th January 1998 - *"Airline Ansett International joined rival air carrier Qantas, in suspending direct services between Australia and South Korea because of the Asian economic meltdown.*

...the airline's twice weekly service to Seoul was no longer commercially viable." End quote.

Australia and New Zealand Loan Korea Money for Bailout

Q. Why? Both of these countries are broke and in deep debt themselves?

A. Because one of the IMF's **conditions** is that everybody helps when called upon.

You can now see the power behind these IMF characters.

'Press', 27th December 1997 - *"New Zealand would lend South Korea up to $100 million to help Korea stabilise and reform its economy.*

The loan followed the International Monetary Fund approach for New Zealand to be part of the bailout package, totalling nearly $US60 billion.

*"It's part of New Zealand **being part of the international financial system**, it's in our interests that Korea bounces back..."*

*...New Zealand has a **"very high" chance** of getting back the $57 million it will lend financially embattled South Korea",* a spokeswoman for the treasurer....says."* End quote.

Author's note - **As much chance as Saddam Hussein has of appearing of the front page of the 'Time' magazine as 'Man of the Year'.**

When a business firm is strapped for cash at the end of the month, which suppliers suffer by not receiving regular payments for their goods and services? The little guys of course. **New Zealand is the little guy on the world trading scene**.

Mind you, they may threaten South Korea like this - "If you don't repay our loan to you, watch out! We'll come after you in our brand new frigate." That should be enough to strike terror into the heart of any nation!

New Zealand Companies Affected

'Dominion', 9th January 1998 - *"Coach company operators are angry about the Government's participation in a bailout of South Korea while, they say, unpaid Korean debts are putting New Zealanders out of work.*

...The drop off in Korean tourism comes on top of an existing problem with Koreans who are considered bad payers.

*...**Within six weeks, about 30 coaches will be repossessed by finance companies**...*

Mr.....believed some of the $57 million earmarked by the Government, should be used to pay debts to New Zealand companies...

*Meanwhile, the Government welcomed formal notification yesterday that **New Zealand is now an approved destination for Chinese tourists**...*"
End quote.

Author's note - This will be okay until the IMF moves in on China with their subtle plans.

A Gold Rush in Reverse

'Korea Times', 13th January 1998 - *"...**Recently, we in Korea have had a reverse type of gold rush**. People, young and old, rich and poor, greedy and not so greedy, are rushing to the banks with all kinds of trinkets for sale, not for profit, but for the payment of debts we owe foreign lenders.*

...In Korea, as in many other Asian countries, everybody knows and nobody denies that every family or individual is hoarding some gold in some way for some purpose.

***Gold** locked in a silver box and kept deep in the safe, may make the hoarder feel better **but it is no longer a good investment**."* End quote.

Author's note on gold - 'Business Herald', 17th December 1997 - *"For thousands of years, gold has been viewed as one of the most precious assets on this earth. It seems to have lost its lustre.*

...One reason for the gold's slump is that central banks have been selling some of their reserves.

*...**The truth is that gold is no longer a monetary asset**.*

...In recent years, governments in Belgium, the Netherlands, Canada, and Australia have sold big chunks of their gold.

...In late October, the gold price dived after a group of experts appointed by the Swiss government proposed that Switzerland sell up 1400 tonnes of gold, more than half its gold reserves..." End quote.

Author's note - Hey! This is a frightening scenario for South East Asians. Gold has always been their foremost commodity in providing security. It is possible that secret planners are changing the goal posts in the middle of the game?

At this moment of writing, I have just remembered an ancient prophecy written about 48 A.D. Listen to the accuracy of it and marvel.

"Go to now ye rich men, weep and howl for your miseries that shall come upon you. Your riches are corrupted, and your garments are motheaten. **Your gold and silver is cankered** *and the rust of them shall be a witness against you, and shall eat your flesh as it were fire.* **You have heaped treasure together for the last days.** *"*[2] End quote.

Could it be possible that as we approach the new millennium that this is indeed the end of an era? The end of life as we have always known it to be. Is some evil power gnawing away at everything we hold dear and everything that has been our security?

Looks like it! Gold is definitely on its way out. Sorry? Read on.

Suicide - A Bad Option

'Samoa News', 30th April 1998 - *"***South Koreans are killing themselves***.*

An average of 25 South Koreans are killing themselves each day as the severe economic downturn demolishes the job security workers enjoyed for more than a decade, according to official figures.

Nearly 2000 people committed suicide in the first three months of this year*, exceeding last year's toll for the same period by 36 per cent, statistics from the National Police Agency reveal.*

....a deepening recession swallows 10,000 jobs a day, pushing unemployment to a 12 year high of 6.5 per cent

In one documented case, a small business owner hanged himself with his wife and son after his business failed.

Last month, four schoolgirls jumped to their deaths from a 20 storey building after complaining of **financial problems***. In another case, a 32 year old man hanged himself after losing his job.*

....the growing tide of **layoffs** *is breeding confusion among workers who never dreamed they would one day be* **jobless***; and depriving them of the status employment brings in this intensely face-conscious nation.*

....Companies are cutting back ruthlessly to survive as the country recovers from a foreign exchange crisis late last year that led to a record bailout from the **International Monetary Fund***....*

Ms Kim said one man who phoned Love Line had **lost his savings in the stock market crash** *and his wife had asked for a divorce.....*

He often roamed the hills around Seoul contemplating suicide." End quote.

The Personal Side of the Korean Tragedy

"South Korea's financial crisis deepened yesterday as the government closed more merchant banks and the country's battered markets dismissed government stabilisation measures.

...For average Koreans, especially those with money in closed merchant banks, the bitterly cold days were filled with despair.

One woman standing outside a closed merchant bank in central Seoul that was ringed by riot police said to anyone who would listen, **"Why won't they give me my money. It's all I have?"** End quote.

The 'Korean Times', 13th January 1998 - *"Rep. Kim Kyung-jae....said.....he wants to devote the rest of his political career to bringing the two Koreas together.*

...Regardless of the economic hardships within the domestic economy (South Korea)...the South should keep providing food aid to the North.

"The situation is different. We are undergoing a temporary economic hardship. However, people are dying of hunger in North Korea...." End quote.

Author's note - Remember at all times, the Hegelian Dialectic -

Thesis - South Korea - Capitalism
Antithesis - North Korea - Communism
Synthesis - New World Order

Thus, we can now clearly see that we are living at a defining stage in history. The **Mystery of Iniquity** is having its surreptitious cover blown.

In spite of this mass of information, the most moving reminder of this South East melt-down may be found on the front page of the 'European' newspaper, 30th October - 5th November 1997. Alongside the large red printed words, **DON'T PANIC**, there is a photograph of a gentleman holding the newspaper stock-market page in his right hand, whilst his left hand covers his mouth. There is a look of shock, horror, and disbelief, that dwarfs any written description of what has just taken place in the South East Asian economic scene.

Reforms in South East Asia

Before we move on to other future trouble spots in South East Asia, let us predict some of the areas in each country to undergo radical change - the catch word of course is **reforms**. This process is what we have been experiencing in New Zealand ever since 1984.

1. Telecommunications must be privatised and sold overseas.

2. Energy Supplies , e.g. Electricity and gas must also be privatised.
3. Transport Infrastructure, Trains, Buses, Airlines - sold
4. Ports and Airports are up for sale. Roads will follow.
5. Welfare will be gradually phased out. Many aspects of law enforcement and jails will be privatised.
6. Voluntary unionism will gradually destroy the collective bargaining structures.
7. All would-be workers will sign personal contracts.
8. Consumption tax, VAT or Goods and Services Tax will be introduced.
9. Education will be in crisis as governments withdraw funding. Private funding of education encouraged.
10. Health and hospitals will suffer the same fate. It just goes on and on.
11. Ex-government department shares will be sold overseas in asset sales. This in turn gradually strips away sovereignty and independence.
12. Local industries that were previously the life blood of the country will collapse. **Deregulation** is the catch word.
13 Each country will be left with only one or two major industries, and will buy in the rest from overseas. The catch word here is **interdependence**.
14. Thus with the protected industry done away with, nobody in the manufacturing business can again feel safe and secure.
15. Farmers will lose their **subsidies** as in most cases, they are targeted for collapse. Food will mostly be imported from somewhere else. The catch word in this case is **interdependence**.

Interdependence

Late in the year 1987, we were giving lectures in the Australian town of Mildura, the orange and grape growing area. Arriving in the town, one of the first things we saw was large convoys of trucks carrying their cargoes of oranges to the local rubbish dumps.

I enquired about what was going on and the locals, speaking in dismayed tones, said, "They are dumping our oranges to make way for imported orange juice from Brazil".

Later, a member of my audience in Great Britain told me that he was from Sweden. In that country, I was told, apple growers in the southern state of the Skane were told by the E.U. to cut down all the good apple trees. The growers were paid in Swedish krona to do so.

The things that have happened in the guinea pig country of New Zealand are also happening all around the world. We know - we are New Zealanders!

Some examples will now make it clear that the **interdependence** plan makes each country responsible for only one or two products:

Scotland - whisky
Great Britain - finance and the social arts
New Zealand - pine logs
South Africa - minerals
Kenya - tourism and safaris
Uganda - coffee
Zambia - copper
Tanzania - diamonds
Germany - luxury cars
Japan - electronics
Switzerland - chocolate, watches and stolen gold
Spain - leather
Canada - wheat for the northern hemisphere
Australia - wheat for the southern hemisphere
Italy - designer clothes
Israel - fruit
Argentina - beef
Sri Lanka - tea - garments
Holland - flower, cheese
Pakistan - cotton
Malaysia - rubber
American Samoa - tuna
Tonga - squash
USA - t.v., Hollywood, coca cola
Brazil - orange juice

Footnotes

[1]   Proverbs 16:9
[2]   James 5:1

CHAPTER FOURTEEN

THE NET EXPANDS

Our particular line of business takes us on constant tours around the world. Sometimes, even three times in the course of one year. An average journey to Great Britain takes about 25 hours, so we normally try to take a break in Bali, Singapore, Kuala-Lumpur or Bangkok.

Singapore used to be good for duty free shopping, but it has now been put to shame by the prices in Bangkok. For example, an average necktie in Singapore costs $40-$60. The same tie in Bangkok costs $3-$4. As I have often explained in my meetings, that is probably one of the reasons they changed the name from Siam to Thailand.

Goodbye Thailand

A previously prosperous country, suddenly brought to its knees! As we examine the media reports on each of these countries, prepare to chuckle with me as we read again the catchwords first practised in New Zealand in the year 1987.

'International Herald Tribune', 6th January 1998 - *"In a new ritual of Thailand's hard times, people who call themselves the 'formerly rich' have been gathering every weekend in a carnival atmosphere to sell their status symbols, expensive cars, designer clothing, thousand-dollar watches, even a light airplane.*

One week, a former employee of a closed finance company hung a "For Sale" sign around his own neck advertising his availability for work....Thailand is emerging from a crippling stage of national denial." Break quote.

Author's note - **Don't laugh overseas readers. Your country is also on the agenda for similar treatment**.

Continue quote - *"...The bad news, analysts say, is that recovery will take time, will cause both economic **pain** and **social disruptions** and will call for **strong political will** among the region's leaders.*

*...In the December report, the Organisation for Economic Cooperation and Development said...in the nearer term, there will be **pain**."* End quote.

New Zealand 'Herald', 9th December 1997 - *"...in the short term the moves are set to be **painful**. There will be a lot of **pain** in the short term. But in five to ten years, they will have secured a whole new financial system",* Dr....said.

*The reality hit hard at firms ordered to close, **with many employees collapsing in tears after the decision to close 56 firms was made public.***

Many of my friends here are crying. Not only have we lost our jobs, but a lot of us have heavy debts like house payments", said an employee." End quote.

'Korea Times', 13ᵗʰ January 1998 - *"...Cash-strapped governments are **tightening their budgetry belts** and it looks like some of the first things to go will be costly military hardware."* End quote.

'Herald', 6ᵗʰ January 1998 - *"In December (1997) the Thai Government said 56 finance companies would be closed down...the good assets are to be disposed of as soon as possible **according to Thailand's agreement with the IMF** and the rest will be flogged off by the end of 1998. But to whom? And at what price?*

...Other obstacles stand in the way of re-establishing a market. Foreigners are still not allowed to own more than a minority share in Thai property." End quote.

Author's note - Notice the **rules.**

1. **Thailand's assets are to be sold up.**
2. **The laws must be changed to allow foreigners to buy into Thailand.**

Now let us look at Indonesia.

Goodbye Indonesia

'Herald', 10ᵗʰ January 1998 - *"Indonesia, which agreed on an IMF-led bailout of over $US40 billion in October, has seen its currency continue to plunge despite the rescue package."* End quote.

'Daily Telegraph', 9ᵗʰ January 1998 - *"Panicking crowds yesterday swamped shops, buying up food and consumer durables as the Indonesian currency plunged to a new low, **less than one quarter of its value six months ago.***

Some banks began to run out of cash because of the number of people withdrawing savings.

*Financial analysts said **confidence** in the rupiah had collapsed because of the government's failure to produce **coherent economic reforms**.*

...The Indonesian economy began its slide last August in the wake of a financial crisis in neighbouring Thailand.

*...In October, the International Monetary Fund negotiated a $38 billion aid package for Indonesia, **on condition** that the government close down insolvent banks and make the rules of business far more transparent."* End quote.

'Press', January 1998 - *"Riots hit several towns in East Java province this week after the basic price of food shot up.*

...The report followed panic buying of food in Jakarta last week, when residents, fearing skyrocketing prices, crammed supermarkets.

*...The military has warned that food hoarders could be charged with **subversion**, which carried the **death penalty**.*

...Hundreds of newspapers may have to stop publishing, the Kompas daily newspaper quoted Indonesia's Newspaper Publisher's Association as saying. The price of a kilogram of paper has increased by 217 per cent..." End quote.

'Herald', 10th January 1998 - *"Widespread hoarding of commodities such as rice, sugar, milk and cooking oil showed the first signs of unease with Indonesia's financial mess..."* End quote.

During the month of May 1998, the country was on the brink of civil war. At last, Suharto resigned.

Welcome to the New World Order.

Goodbye Malaysia

'Sunday Telegraph', 11th January 1998 - *"Malaysian civil servants are being barred from overseas vacations, the nation has been asked to opt for one lump in its tea, to keep imports down and the prison service is to cultivate vegetables and fruit in prison grounds to cut the food bill."* End quote.

'Korean Times', 13th January 1998 - *"Prime Minister, Mahathir Mohamad, said Monday that one million foreign workers would have to return to their countries of origin as Malaysia deals with the current economic crisis.*

...Malaysia has about two million foreign workers, including an estimated one million illegal workers which would account for about ten per cent of the local workforce. Most are from Indonesia, Bangladesh, Thailand and the Philippines." End quote.

Goodbye Taiwan

'Herald', 7th January 1998 - *"One of Asia's so-called Tigers, however, has fared far better than the rest. While Korea and South East Asia are struggling, **Taiwan has so far escaped** with a small currency devaluation and a relatively modest decline in share prices.*

Economic growth remains strong..." End quote.

Prediction - Just wait. Taiwan will be brought down along with the rest. (Written 22nd January 1998.)

Who else is on the proverbial skids?

Goodbye China

So Hong Kong has returned to Mother China. Just in time for a monetary melt-down.

'Korea Herald', 13th January 1998 - *"Hong Kong stock prices plunged 8.7 per cent Monday, foreshadowing the demise of Peregrine Investment Holdings which finally filed for **liquidation** shortly after the market closed.*

... "People are worried about Hong Kong's financial future"....It is a sensitive market waiting for good news and no more bad news..." End quote.

New Zealand 'Herald', 13th January 1998 - *"Seven years after the country (China) established its stock exchanges, its markets are reeling, and so are companies' plans to raise money in them.*

For China, the turmoil could not come at a worse time. Only months ago, Beijing said it would sell shares in its state-run companies, many of which are losing money. Now, that would not be easy, traders say." Break quote.

Author's note - These Chinese Communists are no fools. They understand very clearly the IMF's designs on world domination. In their frantic quest to stay clear of the IMF **conditions**, these cunning characters promised to let foreign investors in, but it is all to no avail. No government on earth can buck the power of the IMF and get away with it.

Continue quote - *"Yesterday, **Chinese shares that foreign investors can own called B shares**, tumbled in Shanghai and Shenzhen, the city just across the border from Hong Kong."*

Christchurch 'Press', 17th January 1998 - *"China has outlined bold steps to avoid a South East Asian style financial crisis, including a sweeping reorganisation of its **creaking banking system** and a plan to clean up bad debt."* End quote.

Goodbye Chinese Communism

'Waikato Times', 27th December 1997 - *"China's leaders ended a three day, closed door, national conference on foreign investment in Beijing this week, and called for **greater efforts to attract foreign investment**, rejecting criticism from die-hard Marxists.*

*State media have recently carried articles by leftists opposed to China **opening its doors to foreign investment** lest foreign ideas creep in and shake the peoples' belief in Communism."* End quote.

Look at this and marvel!

Many of Asia's leaders understand the power behind the IMF **loans and conditions plan**. The powers of perception appear to be sharper than other world leaders, who ran like sheep to the slaughter into the IMF trap.

'Daily Telegraph', 12th January 1998 - *"There were plans in the autumn for Asia to set up a rival monetary fund of its very own. This has been dropped like a hot dim sim as the prospective members realised that the fund would have more borrowers than lenders.*

The IMF is welcome to the job, and its monopoly will not be challenged..." End quote.

By the way, 11 million in China are about to lose their jobs - **redundancy I believe, is the key word!**

It's Worse Than You Think

Christchurch 'Press', 21st January 1998 - *"Anybody returning from an Asian capital these last few months has horror stories of the financial crisis, and how savagely and rapidly it has hit just about every aspect of life.*

...An Auckland marketing man came back from a trip through the region...

In Bangkok, he saw dozens of city building sites abandoned, each of them representing hundreds of workers, now unemployed. The bright side to the story was that the city's notorious traffic jams were not so bad...But that was only a partial blessing because scores of taxis had been abandoned by drivers who couldn't meet the spiralling interest rates on their loans.

In Hong Kong , he said, he talked to real-estate agents dealing in mid-priced apartments, who hadn't made a sale for months..."

In Taiwan he was stunned by the uncertainty that was paralysing even apparently sturdy businesses. All decisions had been put on hold he said.

The story was worse in Seoul, where the crisis had been accompanied by a traditional Korean dose of soul-searching, questioning the path by which Korea emerged from subjugation and poverty to Asian-tiger status in little more than a generation." Break quote.

Author's note - **Please read the next note carefully as it points out once again New Zealand's guinea-pig, test-case status for all these weird and wonderful reforms.**

Continue quote - *"Plenty of critics of New Zealand's own reforms have concluded that it's a case of "told you so", that the economic miracle we are trying to pull off here has collapsed in the countries that were supposed to be our models.*

...People with any experience of business in Asia have been complaining for years about restrictive trade practices, "crazy capitalism" that has closed deals to outsiders, and rigid control of economies by "Think Big" governments.

*The IMF is now **insisting** that as a **condition** for its bailouts, these issues have to be sorted out. This will mean, not just an uncertain future for leaders, such as Indonesia's President Suharto, but very unpleasant **belt-tightening** for ordinary Asians..."* End quote.

You will see what happened. Within a few brief months after this article was written, Suharto was toppled. This however, made not an ounce of difference to Indonesia's financial woes.

The whole plan is very tough on local politicians, who don't wish to resign, nor do they have the intestinal fortitude to tell the truth!

There it is again. **Tighten up the old belts** my friends. Prepare to endure lots of **pain** and look for the elusive **light at the end of the tunnel**!

Japan the Trigger

For many years, Westerners made jokes about Japan and Japanese technology. If it was cheap and easily broken, it was made Japan. I remember watching a man laying concrete blocks on a building site. He was extra rough with his trowel and tried to divide a concrete block with it. Of course, it broke. He looked at it, held it up and muttered one word, "Japanese".

And then, the Japanese came to New Zealand with their expertise and added an extension to Auckland Harbour Bridge. People chuckled as they named it the **Nippon clip-on**, yet even today, it is still handling the traffic flow.

Now, any student of economics knows that Japan is now so powerful on the world trading scene, that it would spell **global catastrophe** if this country experienced a monetary meltdown.

I'm sorry folks but the news is not good.

New Zealand 'Herald', 6th January 1998 - *"It was the year when the secrets come out, spreading an ugly stain across Japan's once proud business reputation.*

...It was also disclosed that corporate racketeers were paid not to disrupt annual meetings with embarrassing questions and the staggering size of reckless bank lending was also revealed.

Weeping company presidents owned up to years of abuse and hiding of bad loans as their firms went bankrupt and they went before the public to confess their wrong-doings.

Along with the financial failures - nine listed firms went bust during the year - died Japan's dreams of becoming a regional leader in Asia, let alone the world.

...Prime Minister....Hashimoto bluntly told Asian Pacific leaders that

"Japan could not be the "locomotive" to pull Asia's other ailing economies out of their mess". His popularity plunged in December to a record low of 30 per cent as the financial meltdown went on.

*...Some analysts believe Mr Hashimoto **may have to resign to clear the way for bolder policy measures**..."* End quote.

Halfway through 1998, he was sacked.

Author's note - What is this? Nothing short of veiled language telling us **the IMF must be allowed in with their loans, conditions, and removal of independence and sovereignty**.

'Press', 20th January 1998 - *"Japan Economy "Sickest".*

Japan is the sickest economy in the world....*a leading U.S. economist said...*

"It (Japan) isn't the poorest, but it is the sickest. It is the sickest because we don't know yet if the South Korean government is good at clearing up the mess, we don't yet know if the Thai Government is good at cleaning up the mess...

*...Dr....said the Japanese had a crash in 1990 which was bigger than the stock market crash in the United States in 1929. **Seven years later, they are still in a mess.**"* End quote.

New Zealand 'Herald', 6th January 1998 - *"Outlook Bleak in Japan.*

A series of polls on Japan's economic outlook show that Japanese business leaders have no illusions about 1998 which they say, will be as bad as 1997 if not worse.

The 'Mainichi Shimbun' newspaper said more than 80 per cent of Japan's leading companies expected the domestic economy to stall or worsen in 1998..." End quote.

The 'European', 30th October-5th November 1997, *"Now the dominoes are falling. **The Japanese recovery - such as it is**, is dependent on exports."* End quote.

'Waikato Times', 13th January 1998 - *"Japanese banks are holding 76.7 trillion ($NZ1.03 billion) in bad and questionable loans - **almost three times the officially reported figure for bad debt**, the Finance Ministry says."* End quote.

'International Herald Tribune', 6th January 1998 - *"Japan's economy, the world's second largest, is growing, its stock and real-estate markets are in the cellar and its banks are buried in bad loans. **Consumer confidence is faltering, corporate bankruptcies are at record levels and the jobless rate** is creeping to a past World War II high.*

And just as in 1990, prospects for recovery are murky.

...government officials around the world are wondering whether the giant Japanese economy....might be in danger of collapse." End quote.

Korea 'Times', January 1998 - *"(Prime Minister) Hashimoto repeated his well-worn phrase to parliament, "I would never let Japan trigger a global financial crisis or economic crisis".* End quote.

Author's note - Actually, this dear man, in his obvious sincerity, was not aware of the forces he was up against.

Haunting Words

His words will come back to haunt him. The videos will play and mockingly replay this statement, over and over again.

Goodbye Japan

"Japan faces crunch time, say analysts." (See article below.)

We have noted the analogy of the link-up of Korea and New Zealand. We have seen that if one collapses, it affects the other. The link between Korea and Japan is far more serious again.

Earthquake

For years, we have pointed out that a severe earthquake in **Tokyo, Japan,** could set off an economic slide, as could a severe shake in California. We can be sure of this, that **if an earthquake does not do the job, our conspiratorial friends will!** They are working hard on South East Asia at this time of writing (January 1998), and their aim is to have every country up to their eyes in debt, and fulfilling the **reforms** by the year 2000. Let us now see what is predicted for Japan.

Japan - The Main Event

'Waikato Times', 10.11.97 - *"Japan's economy is sliding towards a crisis that will dwarf Southeast Asia's troubles, and there are few escape hatches, analysts say.*

The East Asian economic crisis was "the sideshow before the real event - the main event is being prepared for you in Tokyo today," said....analyst at Deutsche Morgan Grenfell.

...The slump has brought the capital adequacy levels of Japanese banks - which rely heavily on equities - to below levels required by the Basel-based Bank for International Settlements..." Break quote.

Author's note - Please obtain a copy of our third book "Final Notice", page 243, for a more in depth explanation on this little publicised group. An understanding of this is important as they also control the World Bank and the I.M.F.

Continue quote - *"This is the panic selling before the crisis forces the Government to abandon its Hooverite policies," said Mr ....., referring to the move by then U.S. president Herbert Hoover to raise taxes during economic recession **leading to the Great Depression of 1929**.*

*...Without government action, an economic crisis in Japan would put the skids under global markets, because **Japan is after all the world's principal source of capital**," the analyst said.*

If the main source of capital goes into a tailspin, watch out.

...The stock market's fall was triggered, he said, by a report that Japan's largest regional bank, Bank of Yokohama, planned to sell its cross-shareholdings..." Break quote.

Author's note - There you go. These are the scare tactics that cause people to lose confidence.

Continue quote - *"Earlier the Japanese finance minister shrugged off concerns over the slack economy, pointing to "progress" in promoting **deregulation**..."* End quote.

This word 'deregulation' is jargon for opening up the markets ultimately to overseas investors. There is no doubt about it - Japan is now on the skids!

G10 Bankers Hopeful

New Zealand 'Herald', 14th January 1998 - *"...Group of Ten central-bank governors, meeting in Basle, were hopeful that **confidence** in all shaken Asian economies would be restored soon..."* End quote.

Now, remember, confidence can only be restored when the IMF come in on the deal with their:

a) Loans
b) Conditions
c) Loss of sovereignty scam.

CHAPTER FIFTEEN

LINKS IN A CHAIN

Asian Crisis Hits Other Countries

New Zealand, U.S.A., Hawaii, Australia and other countries are now being mentioned in our media reports as suffering hardship. This is all a result of the melt-down in South East Asia.

'Sunday Star Times', 25th January 1998 - *"For long enough, it was just an academic debate. Is New Zealand to be part of Asia, or should it regard itself as just a South Pacific nation close to Asia but no more part of it than it is of Europe or America?*

However much New Zealanders may like to be spectators of the Asian economic crisis, the collateral damage hit home last week.

*...**The tourist flow from South Korea** which last year brought 125,000 visitors and $230 million has dried up. **Tourist traffic out of Thailand** (240,000 visitors last year) and **Indonesia** (14,000 last year) is also virtually at a standstill.*

...New Zealand needs investment of $75-$100 billion over the next five years to maintain this decade's economic and employment growth.

...International Trade Minister, Dr...noted that the difficulty for us is that figures like $100 billion are clearly beyond the savings of fewer than four million people." Break quote.

Author's note - The New Zealand population stands at 3½ million.

Continue quote - *"So we have a choice. We either restrict our investment pool to that held by New Zealanders...or we can continue to attract investment from overseas."* End quote.

Author's note - An English paraphrase of what this gentlemen is really trying to say, but failing badly in the process, is - **"Because five men in New Zealand's Labour Party collaborated to sell up the assets of the State-owned Enterprises (SOE's), our country is suffering."** For this reason, we desperately need overseas investors to keep our country afloat.

From 1987 onwards therefore, along with the selling up of these money-making assets, went any possible hope of this country continuing to exist as an independent state or unit.

Some of the New Zealand politicians in power knew this to be a fact, and it was for this reason that they frantically tried to rush through the

OECD plan called MAI - Multilateral Agreement on Investment." They did not initially succeed but they will certainly try again as soon as possible. This is what the man meant when he spoke of the need for investment from overseas.

Christchurch 'Press', 26th January 1998 - *"Business has slumped to its lowest level in seven years...*

*The sharpest falls in confidence were among **manufacturers, merchants and builders**...*

"Christmas did not come for merchants".

*...Uncertainty about the Asian financial crisis, its timing and impact on New Zealand seemed to have **"spooked"** businesses."* End quote.

Christchurch 'Press', 24th January 1998 - *"Trading with Asia worsens almost by the hour for many New Zealand exporters.*

*Problems are occurring for some of the countries biggest export industries - **dairying, forestry, and now wool** - as well as for niche ones such as **deer velvet**.*

*...The dairy board has increased its Jakarta accounting staff to cope with credit problems. It is stopping supplies to stores and chains that cannot pay in **United States dollars**."* .

Australia Suffering

'Sydney Morning Herald', 14th January 1998 - *"Fears are mounting that the Asian economy crisis could lead to a sharp downturn in growth and even recession in Australia.*

...Collectively they (the Asian countries) are about 60 per cent of our exports.

...Australia has a much larger exposure to the Asian region than the U.S. with about two-thirds of exports going to the region, compared with just over ten per cent for the U.S.

*Concern about the Asian impact on Australia resurfaced in the currency market yesterday after **an International Monetary Fund report said New Zealand was at risk** because of its high foreign debt and current account deficit."*

Hawaii Suffering

'Fiji Times', 6th January 1998 - *"Asia Crisis Hits Hawaii.*

Recession is a phenomenon which at first glance does not seem to have any place in a holiday paradise such as Hawaii. But recession has found a place here.

ANNOUNCING THE BIRTH OF THE NEW WORLD
ORDER (WITHOUT GOD), UNDER THE ALL-
SEEING EYE OF SATAN, THE ANTI-CHRIST,
666

...The change began in the early 1980's, the time of the great Japanese invasion.

The Japanese arrived with great dreams, still greater briefcases bursting at the seams. One of the arrivals was Genshiro Kawamoto, a billionaire from Tokyo. In 1987, he allowed himself to be chauffeured along Kahala Avenue in a Rolls Royce.

Kahala is the most expensive residential street in Hawaii and as he was driven along it, Kawamoto bought 170 houses. He literally bought them as he was driven past.

Today, the property in another up-market street, Kalakaua Avenue, the boulevard is 90 per cent in Japanese hands.

...Super rich Japanese came and bought houses on the island of Oahu at double the going rate, immediately tore them down and replaced them with pompous marble villas.

...In 1990...the state, which was a huge sugar cane and pineapple plantation, went through a change.

Today, sugar and pineapple provide only one per cent of Hawaii's Gross Domestic Product (GDP) while 40 per cent comes from tourism and 11 per cent from the Pentagon, which maintains 46 military bases on seven islands.

*Today, the boom is a thing of the past. The great awakening came at the latest with Iniki. Paradise is now even too expensive for the Japanese and **too full of risks as they look again at the yen. The tourist tide is ebbing**.*

Many Japanese are instead looking at the much cheaper island of Guam, which is also in the Pacific but which can be reached even more quickly than Hawaii. And for many Americans, Las Vegas is suddenly more attractive and exciting than Hawaii.

In addition, Hawaii has the highest tax rates of all the 50 U.S. States...."
End quote.

America Suffering

'International Herald Tribune', 6th January 1998 - *"U.S. Booms along Shadowed by Nervousness.*

So far, the Asian financial crisis has hit Boeing Co. with all the force of a wispy feather.

*...Behind that picture of good fortune, however, is a **disquieting fear**. Nearly one third of Boeing's backlog of orders are from Asian airlines. If they began to cancel, Boeing would be in trouble.*

The U.S. economy**, like so many of its premier companies **is in a similar

position. *There is plenty to celebrate but the boom is precarious.*

*...People are talking of the **domino effect**. If Korea and Japan are down, who are we in America to think that our economy can grow?"* End quote.

Japan Suffering

'International Herald Tribune', 6th January 1998 - "*Will Japan Drag Itself Out of the Doldrums?*

*Japan's economy, the world's second largest is barely growing, its stock and real-estate markets are in the cellar and its banks are buried in bad loans. **Consumer confidence is falling**, corporate bankruptcies are at record levels, and the **jobless rate** is creeping to a post-World War II high.*

And, just as in 1990, prospects for recovering are murky.

*...**Financial crises elsewhere in Asia have prompted investors and government officials around the world to wonder whether the giant Japanese economy, too, might be in danger of collapse**.*" End quote.

Author's note - There is really no need to wonder any longer. **It must and will collapse at the right time. And thus, the U.S. and other world economies will follow suit.**

A Key Statement

There are no accidents in this planned collapse of the nations. Everything is carefully organised. Who is the organiser again?

CHAPTER SIXTEEN

THE U.S. ROLE IN THE CONSPIRACY

Bill Blythe Will Continue with the New World Order Plan

Young Bill's father, William Jefferson Blythe III, had been killed in an automobile accident before Bill was born, so Virginia Blythe carried the responsibility of raising him as a single mother.

In 1950, Virginia Blythe married Roger Clinton from Hot Springs, Arkansas, and that is when young Bill got his new name.

At school, he was an active student politician, and belonged to the **Masonic order - DeMolay. He attended the Park Place Baptist church. Later he became a Rhodes Scholar, and a Yale law school graduate.**

Author's notes -

a. The Baptist Church in the U.S.A. does not make an open stand against Freemasonry and its pagan beliefs.
b. Cecil Rhodes devoted his life to a Global government. Rhodes Scholars therefore are trained in international thinking.
c. The motto of Yale University is the same as that on the US$1 bill - Novus Ordo Seclorum - A secular, godless, one world government.

Ice-cream - Young Bill loved ice-cream and barbecues. He ate his Cooks ice-cream at this address - 314 Albert Pike.

Barbecues - He ate his barbecues at McLand's Bar-B-Que at this address - 505 Albert Pike.

Freemasons - He served as Master Counsellor of DeMolay while in high school. He also received his degree of Chevalier, which is the highest honour an active DeMolay can receive.

Fact - Within 9 hours of the shooting of President John F. Kennedy in Dallas, Texas, just when the investigation had barely begun, the t.v. networks announced that the shooting was not a conspiracy - why? Had somebody suspected it may have been?

Readers of our fifth book, 'Better Than Nostradamus', however, will have read the examining doctor's testimony. He was instructed to say the bullet entered Kennedy's head from the back, and was to doctor up the wound to make this credible. He later confessed that **the bullet came from the front**.

This is why Jackie tried to climb out the rear of the car and not the side, as any normal person would have done.

Fact - The people who lived at the Branch-Davidian headquarters at Waco, Texas, did not commit suicide.

They were shot, and then set on fire by agents of the U.S. government. This is quite clear as one views the video, 'Waco - the Big Lie'. The viewer can watch government agents apparently shooting their own men. Then the final indignity is added when they bring in flame-throwers to ignite the deadly C2 gas.

It is actually sickening to watch.

Fact - This author has in his possession a copy of a letter providing irrefutable proof that the Oklahoma bombing was not solely caused by a truck bomb.

This letter, along with the enclosed report mentioned (see below), written in full, was sent to Senator Trent Lott, United States Senate, on 30th July, 1995.

"Dear Senator Lott

*The attached report contains conclusive proof that the bombing of the Alfred P. Murrah Federal Building, Oklahoma City, Oklahoma, was **not caused solely by the truck bomb**.*

*Evidence shows that the massive destruction was primarily the result of **four demolition charges** placed at critical structural points at the **third floor level**..."* End quote.

A Brigadier General, Benton R. Partin, USAF (Ret) reports (in part) *"....some of the columns collapsed that should not have collapsed if the damage were caused solely by a truck bomb, and conversely, some of the columns were left standing that should have collapsed if the damage had been caused solely by the truck bomb.*

*...No government law enforcement agency should be permitted to demolish, smash, or bury evidence of a counter-terrorism sting operation, sabotage, or terrorist attack without a thorough investigation **by an independent**, technically competent agency.*

*...It is my observation that the effort required to bomb the AP Murrah Federal Building in Oklahoma City pales in comparison withe **the effort to cover up evidence in Oklahoma and the media's withholding of vital information** from the American people..."* End quote.

I don't know how this information strikes you, but I find it thoroughly nauseating. I sometimes wish that I had not become involved in all this as the **more you learn, the dirtier the picture becomes.** The average person does not have access to the masses of information that arrives daily at our office. However, remember the old adage - 'Don't believe everything you read'. In view of today's expanded information sources, it should be extended to 'Don't believe everything you read, whether it be the newspaper or the world wide web.'

Check, and triple check is the name of this game!

As a boy, my Dad pointed out to me that the devil's greatest weapon was to convince humanity that he doesn't exist e.g. How much of this information did you know about before you read it in this chapter?

	No	Yes
Kennedy's Death	☐	☐
Waco Murders	☐	☐
Oklahoma Bombing	☐	☐

Fact - Did you know, for example, that ex-president, George Bush, belonged to an ultra-secret, non-American society, called the 'Skull and Bones', whilst he was studying at Yale University. Only two writers seem to know anything about this odd group of **surreptitious grave-robbers i.e. Ron Rosenbaum and Antony Sutton**.

Within the vaults of their society, the Bonesmen are said to have the skull of the legendary Indian chief, Geronimo.

Antony C. Sutton, in his outstanding book entitled 'The Order', on page 322, gives us some interesting insights into this spooky establishment. The preface to this book is absolutely fascinating. (By the way, you are not reading the ramblings of one, Mr Michael Mouse, from Disney World on these pages.)

Mr Sutton was a research Fellow at the Hoover Institution, Stanford University, from 1968 to 1973. He is a former economics professor at California State University, Los Angeles.

He was born in London in 1925 and educated at the universities of London, Gottingen, and California and has written at least 17 other books besides 'The Order'.

I invite you to come along with me and check out some of his observations. The date - 30th January 1998.

In the 'Author's Preface, An Introduction to the Order', he talks about his previously written books.

*"These volumes explain **why** the West built the Soviets and Hitler, **why** we go to war to lose, **why** Wall St loves Marxists and Nazis, **why** the kids can't read, **why** the churches have become propaganda founts, **why** historical facts are suppressed, **why** politicians **lie** and a hundred other **whys**."* End quote.

I list below some of the conclusions Mr Sutton comes to.

1. *"There is a massive conspiracy still being conducted in the U.S.A. today."* (Author's note - If you do not believe this, ask yourself how Bill Clinton stayed so long in power.) *"Proof of a conspiracy requires specific types of evidence.*

   A. *There must be **secret** meetings of the participants, and efforts made to conceal joint actions.*

   B. *Those meetings must jointly agree to take a **course of action**.*

   C. *And the action must be **illegal**."* End quote.

2. Chapter 322 "*(The Order)...is a **secret** society, whose members are sworn to silence.*

   *...Above all, **The Order is powerful, unbelievably powerful**.*

   ...The Order meets annually - patriarchs only - on Deer island in the St Lawrence River.

   *...The most likely potential member is from a Bones family (322 or Order)...**A man who will sacrifice himself for the good of the team**...In real life, the thrust of the Order is to bring about certain objectives."* End quote.

   Author's note - Under the New World Order plan, Presidents, Prime Ministers and finance ministers, must be prepared to sacrifice themselves as they implement IMF conditions.

3. Another comment - *"When a new member is initiated in The Order, "Tonight he will die to the world and be **born again into The Order**", as he will thenceforth refer to it. The Order is a world unto itself in which he will have a new name and fourteen new blood brothers, also with new names..."* End quote.

   Author's note - Ex-President, George Bush, holds our immediate interest as being the gentleman who first publically introduced the New World Order in 1990. He also spoke of the 1000 Points of Light, or the many groups involved in setting up the **One World Government**. His new name **given to him by The Order - "Poppy"**.

Using the term "born again", in this manner is a satanic twisting of the truth of this truly outstanding experience. Jesus spoke of it as a necessity for any who have Heaven as their ultimate goal i.e. "You must be born again."[1]

4. *"There exists in the United States today, and has existed since 1833, a secret society comprising members of old line American families and representatives of financial power.*

5. ***The Order*** *has penetrated or been the dominant influence in sufficient policy, research and opinion making organisations that it **determines the basic direction of American society.***" End quote.

Very Important

6. *"The activities of The Order are directed towards changing our society, changing the world, to bring about a New World Order. This will be a planned order, with **heavily restricted** individual freedom, without Constitutional protection, **without national boundaries** or cultural distinction.*

*...Historically, operations of The Order have concentrated on **society**, how to change society in a specific manner towards a specific goal, a New World Order.*

We know the elements in society that will have to be changed in order to bring about this New World Order, we can then examine The Order's actions in this context." End quote.

(Remember, A. Sutton's book was first printed in 1985.)

More or less, these elements have to be:

- ***"Education*** *- how the population of the future will behave.*
- ***Money*** *- the means of holding wealth and exchanging goods.*
- ***Law*** *- the authority to enforce the will of the state. A world law, and a world court is needed for a world state. John Dewey, the American educationalist, believed that man has no individual rights. He is only there to serve the State.*
- ***Politics*** *- the direction of the State.*
- ***Economy*** *- the creation of wealth.*
- ***History*** *- what people believe happened in the past.*
- ***Psychology*** *- the means of controlling how people think and affect behaviour - media, t.v.*
- ***Philanthropy*** *- so that people think well of the controllers.*
- ***Medicine*** *- the power over health, life and death.*
- ***Religion*** *- peoples' spiritual beliefs, the spur to action for many.*
- ***Media*** *- what people learn and know about current events.*

- *Continuity* - *the power to appoint who follows in your footsteps."* End quote.

Method of Operation - Hegelian Logic

Remember again the German philosopher, Hegel.

You will be interested to know, the extremes of **left** and **right**, **Marx** and **Hitler**, evolved out of this system.

...**This conflict of opposites is essential to bring about change.**

Today in most countries on earth, the key words "**change**", and "**conflict management**" helps to bring about this change.

Another word to remember is "**internationalism**" which involves "**global organisation**" and "**world law**".

As I continue writing this book, I feel it would be an appropriate time to take careful stock of Antony Sutton's information. We will look at each area in February 1998 and see what progress has been made.

    1998
    <u>-1985</u>
    13 years later.

Summary

Education - How the population of the future will behave.

Fulfilment - Many older people can remember those 'better days' when children :
- respected their elders.
- sat in straight rows in class and learned something.
- knew their times tables and the alphabet.
- learned to read using phonics and syllabification.
- looked neat and tidy when they attended school.
- had their nails examined and their hair neatly brushed.
- honoured their families.
- honoured their country and flag.
- stood quietly at school assemblies for hymn singing and prayer to Almighty God (the Father of the Lord Jesus Christ.)
- boys did not swear in the presence of girls.
- children stood up for their elders on buses and trams etc.
- because there were no t.v.'s or computer games, the children could manage to smile and put a few words together in the form of a sentence when asked a question. In other words, the majority were not brain dead as many unfortunately are today.

- read books, and had a knowledge of the countries of the world and of the history of their particular nation.

Many older people can remember those 'better days' when:

- musicians looked like **normal people** and not like the village idiot. They did not need to wear dark glasses on dull days as most of their work was performed indoors and the majority of them were not blind. They realised a very basic truth i.e. in order to be a musician, all that was required was for them to play music. Simple, wasn't it?
- the boys kept their hair neatly trimmed and would never think of wearing an ear-ring. There was nothing worse than the stigma of looking like a girl or a weirdo.
- music had a tune to it which one could whistle or sing. It was structured music that went somewhere and had a satisfactory, satisfying ending to each verse.
- peer pressure to conform kept people in a community thoughtful of the group as a whole - **consideration** was the key word.
- boys were encouraged to be boys and girls to be girls. Everybody knew that God created just these two gender groups and that anything else was **abnormal**.
- discipline was enforced at school and at home with the cane or the strap. Normal thinking people were smart enough to see that one good whack over the rear end was quicker and more useful than a thousand words of discussion.
- psychologists were not in vogue as normal people knew instinctively the difference between **discipline** and **violence**.

Q. What went wrong? Do you sincerely believe all this change for the worse is any accident or a quirk of nature?

A. No! It is not an accident. Antony Sutton, in 'The Order', points out the following: *"The look and say (**look and guess**) reading method was designed for deaf mutes. After all, a citizen who cannot read or write is not going to challenge The Order.*

*...It is apparently of no concern to the educational establishment that children can't read, can't write and can't do elementary mathematics...but they **are** going to be ready for a Brave New World."* End quote.

Money - Prediction - the means of holding wealth and exchanging goods.

Fulfilment - During a lecture tour to Sri Lanka in the year 1997, it was so odd to see cash being used on every hand. Of course, coming from the test case, guinea-pig country of New Zealand where **cash transactions** are looked upon with the **utmost suspicion**, I had forgotten how far we had advanced.

New Zealand is far, far, more advanced in the cashless, electronic system than for example, the U.S.A. In many areas in that country, you still have to transfer your money or cheques by mail.

Now, in the country of New Zealand, all the banks are working on a common data base, which means that those in authority can access any citizen's account at will.

Some years ago, whilst holding lectures in Auckland city, a man approached me and passed on the following information - "I attend all your lectures, Barry, because I know what you are saying is correct."

When questioned further, he told me the following. "I hold a managerial position with a major plastic card company. We no longer need a James Bond character wearing a cap, dark glasses and collar turned up. All we need, is a customer with one of our plastic cards. With the press of a button, we know which country he is in, which hotel he is staying at, his favourite restaurants, his reading habits, the clubs he visits, his telephone habits, the car he hires, where he stops for petrol and oil. If necessary, we can delve deeper into his private lifestyle. Always remember", he went on, "All this goes on the computer and **the computer never forgets**'!'

Secondly, in this decade, many older people in many countries, whose governments are at present adopting and following to the letter, the **Kiwi Experiment**, (as an Australian newspaper labelled it), are in for a **nasty shock**.

Assets Testing

Any person in the future applying for superannuation, benefits or welfare assistance, will need first of all, to furnish the government with a complete list of their assets. This list will include - houses, cars, boats, caravans, blankets, pictures, knives, forks, spoons, vases, carpets, drapes, tools, equipment - viz. everything! The computer then does a comparison check on what you have declared in your annual tax statement and your assets.

Should there prove to be a discrepancy, **oh dear**. You hear footsteps coming up the path, a knock at your door, and there stands your friendly government inspector, with a very official looking document in his hand.

You have been sprung! Why do you think it is that many of the **big boys** in business are getting caught out these days. Reason - the electronic computerised system searches into every nook and cranny and leaves little room for manoeuvring.

Elderly people in other countries - take a friend's advice. Beat the World Government's Dirty Tricks Department and withdraw your cash savings from the bank and **as long as cash remains in vogue**, go back to the old fashioned system for saving. It is called CIS - i.e. Cash in Sock.

Law - Prediction - the authority to enforce the will of the state - a world law and a world court is needed for a world state. On 21st July 1998, 120 countries agreed to a World Criminal Court. This is the thin end of the wedge. The U.S. abstained.

Fulfilment - Some years ago whilst on a lecture tour of Australia, the headline news involved the Franklin High Dam in Australia. At that stage, every Australian state was autonomous and made their own decisions.

Suddenly, for the first time in Australia's short history, the Federal Government stepped in and interfered with a state decision.

Why? Australia was a signatory to a world government environmental treaty from overseas.

Don't Rock the Boat

In the world of politics, the man who tries to be an individualist in the years leading up to the year 2000 is preparing to cut his own political throat. Upon arriving at the hallowed halls of parliament, these persons are quietly taken aside and the rules explained.

Always remember that one of the main rules for members of **The Order** is - never try to do it by yourself. **We are looking for team members.** This is the **global challenge.**

Secure the Job

A friend and ex-politician told me of the joys of having M.P. (Member of Parliament) after your name. Free cars, free travel by air, special treatment at airports.

What does one have to do to receive all these 'perks'? Attend parliament as regularly as possible, speak up on some issue or other, and keep your name before the public via the media. For example, at this time of writing, our province is experiencing what I believe to be one of the worst droughts in history. Our local politician, when approached by affected farmers for help, wrinkled his brow and then said "**It is clear that we are going through a very serious period**", or words to that effect.

In order to stay in power, each government member must remember to always ratify United Nations Charters as they come through i.e. Human rights, the rights of the child, the environment, etc etc, until our national law becomes subservient to international law.

You were correct once more, Mr Sutton.

Politics - **Prediction** - the direction of the State.

Fulfilment - in earlier chapters of this book, we have established that as the national assets are sold overseas, following the **IMF loans-conditions-selling out sovereignty plan**, politicians are left giving the illusion that they are in charge, but simply fulfilling the IMF conditions and handing out sweet treats to the group that shouts the loudest, hoping to quieten them down.

Sad, yet very true. This is in no way a criticism of any parliamentarian. Many will not even realise the trap they are in until they read a book like this.

Economy - **Prediction** - the creation of wealth.

Fulfilment - under the New World Order plans now being implemented, big business i.e. those who have the funds wave the carrot of support under the government of the day's nose, and certain policies are immediately implemented.

Insider knowledge is most important, and as state-owned enterprises are sold up, which persons do you suppose are assisted in buying up massive proportions of the national shareholding at **mate's rates**? Why, government members and their big business advisor mates.

Before New Zealanders became aware that sheep and cattle farming was to be down-graded, and the country planted out in pine trees, I stood alongside a New Zealand politician and did a little eaves-dropping. "I've just bought myself a good stand of pine forest", I heard him whisper to his friend.

I was mystified at the time, as pines were a dime a dozen. It was later revealed that under the New World Order plan, New Zealand's role was to provide pine trees for the global village.

The reason for this was clear, because along with Chile, which is on the same latitude as New Zealand, pine trees grow faster here than anywhere else in the world.

Thus, as we approach the new millennium, the 'pawns', the 'cannon fodder' known as the nobodies of society, are gradually pauperised and kept entertained with raffles, bingo, and multi-channel t.v. with plenty of sport - the middle class is taxed into pacified submission, while the rich rake it in and expand their already bulging bank accounts.

...Later of course, when the extremely wealthy have salted away much of their earnings in tax havens overseas, they receive insider advice from friends in high places on the state of the national economy. When things look bad for the future, they sprout wings like doves and fly away with their money to warmer climes.

Where did we read this quote again? *"Whatsoever a man soweth, that shall he also reap"*.[2] End quote.

An ancient prophecy springs to mind at this juncture. Written in approximately 48 A.D. *"Go to now, ye rich men, weep and howl for your miseries that shall come upon you. Your riches are corrupted, and your garments are motheaten. Your gold and silver is cankered, and the rust of them shall be a witness against you, and shall eat your flesh as it were fire. Ye have heaped treasure together for the last days."*[3] End quote.,

Author's note - Someone reading this article throws his head back and with a knowing chuckle says, "This will never happen in my lifetime!"

Won't it? Ask the previously wealthy in South East Asia. I recently heard of a South Korean director of a large conglomerate that failed. Mr Ho is now out on the streets selling hot-dogs.

However, the prophecy is not finished. Let us read on a passage that deals with unscrupulous businessmen that have no feelings for their workers as they send them down the road. It used to be called **"getting the sack"**, **but today it is "structural readjustment".**

"Behold, the hire of the labourers who have reaped down your fields, which is of you kept back by fraud, crieth, and the cries of them which have reaped are entered into the ears of the Lord of the Sabbaoth. Ye have lived in pleasure on the earth, and been wanton, ye have nourished your hearts, as in a day of slaughter."[4] End quote.

A rather clear explanation I feel, of what awaits those who rode rough-shod over the working public.

'South West Africa' newspaper, January 1998 - *"A Hong Kong science teacher, still clutching his share certificates, leapt 28 floors to his death after losing his savings in the stock market's recent plunge. Yu Keung-lun jumped from a list lobby window in a Hong Kong industrial district. The local market had shed about 40 per cent of its value since early August and many Hong Kong people are believed to have lost tens of thousands of dollars"*. 'Media Windhoek', S.W. Africa.

History - Prediction - what people believe happened in the past.

Fulfilment - A watering down of unpalatable facts is part of the deal.

For example, there are some very uninformed persons in society who try to convince us that the Nazi extermination programme of the Jews never really took place.

One visit to the Holocaust Museum in Israel should do the trick.. If this is not possible, listen to the terrible story of a Jewish survivor who has a number indelibly tattooed on his arm.

Fortunately, only a tiny minority swallow this obvious deception, yet sadly, the story is still doing the rounds.

You see, ultimately, Adolf Hitler and Pol Pot could be viewed as **humanitarians** who were simply assisting in the task of population control. This in turn would assist the world to be a more pleasant place for the rest of us to live.

Please do not mock this last statement. You possibly do not have access to material on this subject, but Jimmy Carter's Global 2000 policies did take the subject very seriously.

The lie is being promulgated in some areas that the world is overpopulated and that we will not have enough land or food to provide for all. Forget it. It is downright deception! The Creator knew what He was doing when He made this world.

Psychology - Prediction - the means of controlling how people think.

Fulfilment - we now live in an age where many folk are involved in **mind games** - mind power - mind over matter - psychology.

We read regular reports of charlatans posing as counsellors who, in order to earn their keep, make suggestions to their patients and thus plant thoughts of things which never happened. It is a dangerous, destructive system, but they persist on and on until their lie is believed and another family is destroyed.

During my school-teaching days, I remember a girl standing up in assembly and before the whole school, called one of the female teachers a **fat old bag**.

During morning tea in the staffroom, I enquired as to what was going to be done about this horrific outburst of venom, against a teacher who was simply trying to do her job.

The counsellor stood up, faced me and said, "Barry, I don't think you quite understand. We need to find out what caused the girl to behave like this."

I replied, "Actually, I'm not interested in why she did it. I just want to make sure she doesn't do it again!"

Sequel - A couple of weeks later, a class came into my room and one of the girls approached me with a very distressed look on her face. She said, "Mr Smith, can you please help me? I was a little bit naughty in my last class and Mr....(the same school counsellor) kicked me in the bottom!"

In the staffroom after school, I told this story to a colleague and finished up by saying "Our psychological counsellor probably examines himself on his own couch at the end of each day."

Wasn't it King Solomon who said, *"Foolishness is bound up in the heart of a child, but the rod of correction shall drive it far from him."*[5] End quote.

Notice how behaviourists think today. Their logical reasoning powers seem to have been taken away. **It is now vogue to equate discipline as violence**. The catch phrase being bandied around today is "violence begets violence". Actually, Solomon was correct again when he said, *"The rod and reproof give wisdom, but a child left to himself bringeth his mother to shame."*[6]

I personally agree with the person who said, "When rearing a child, throw Dr Spock's book in the fire, and turn to the book of Proverbs given to Solomon by Almighty God."

Dr Spock, who passed away during the year 1998, made some outrageous statements e.g. "If your child misbehaves in public, there is nothing you can do about it. You must grin and bear it."

Philanthropy - Prediction - so that people think well of the controllers.

Fulfilment - Politicians know only too well the power of money.

An extract taken from 'The Handwriting on the Wall' by David Jeremiah (pg 62) - "A democracy cannot exist as a permanent form of government. It can only exist until the voters discover that they can vote themselves money from the public treasury.. From that moment on, the majority always votes for the candidates promising the most money from the public treasury, with the result that democracy always collapses over loose fiscal policy followed by a **dictatorship**.

Author's note - Believe me, this world will soon be controlled by a one man dictatorship. Hitler was a **forerunner** or **prototype** of this future world leader.

Antichrist is his title!

Medicine - Prediction - the power over health, life and death.

Fulfilment - In the late 19th century, chemical-based medicine was introduced and the medical profession cut its ties with naturopathy - cancer statistics tell you the rest.

The apocalyptic prophecy found in the book of Revelation gives a list of those who are denied entrance to the holy city. *"But without are dogs, and **sorcerers**, and whoremongers, and murderers, and idolators, and whosoever loveth and maketh a lie."*[7] End quote.

The Greek word which has been translated 'sorcerers' in English is 'pharmakeia' or 'pharmacy' or 'pharmaceuticals'. In clear English therefore, it would appear that the pharmaceutical drug trade could be connected in some way with sorcery or witchcraft.

I personally find it very sad that in some countries the medical authorities who set the rules on legal treatments and therapies sometimes have vested financial interests in the pharmaceutical companies. Thus, any non-chemical treatment is immediately given the thumbs down, even if its efficacy has been proved beyond a shadow of a doubt to be beneficial.

Bad News

There is even a move afoot, early in the year of 1998, to make it compulsory for naturopaths and alternative health practitioners to come under the umbrella of a the Drug Administrators and the authoritative Medical Associations of each country. This is a dangerous precedent as it will turn many good living people into criminals simply because they chose natural methods instead of pharmaceutical drugs.

And someone has the audacity to tell me that there is no devil. Well, I'll tell you what. Someone else is doing his work for him!

These individuals in high places have a lot to answer for. First they legalise the killing of the unborn child (abortion) then they twist and squirm through the law courts until it becomes legal to kill others they feel need to be put down (euthanasia).

Meanwhile, in the intervening period between birth and death, they find it economically advantageous to tell us what to take as remedies for our sicknesses.

It's not on!

Religion - Prediction - peoples' spiritual beliefs, the spur to action for many.

Fulfilment - It has been said that man is incurably religious. Bob Dylan summed this up in his song where he said (or possibly attempted to sing), "You've gotta serve somebody".

The **ancient adage - nothing begets nothing**, does not only appeal to the non-intellectual thinker, but also to the person who can accept, with humility the point, that a work of exquisite design of necessity also requires a designer.

Evolution is well-known today to be an out-dated fad, promoted in a half-hearted way by one **Charles Darwin**. In his writings, he made it clear that he was merely **thinking aloud**. He was surprised and shocked when it took on like a religion, for that is exactly what it was and is.

It is simply the anti-God establishments's **pitiful replacement** theory for the origins of everything we know exists both in this world, and beyond.

A sincere evolutionist, if there is really such a being, possibly needs to purchase a copy of the 'Gaia Peace Atlas' and read this portion of the Introduction.

*"The scientist, James Lovelock, believing that life on other planets could be detected by its impact on atmospheric chemistry, turned his attention to Earth and found its **atmosphere so "improbable" in geochemical terms that only some regulatory process could explain it.***

The "regulator" he proposed was life, planetary life as a whole self-regulating organism. He named this entity Gaia, after the ancient Greek goddess of the earth..." End quote.

Hello-hello-hello....

First they said it was an accidental cosmic 'big bang', when we all began to evolve from nothing. Of course, anybody who studies flowers, or birds for example, finds problems on every hand.

I really enjoyed a programme on television recently where it showed a bird with a great curved beak. Alongside, the bird was a great curved flower that the bird sucked the nectar from. Initially of course, the bird said, "My beak is not the right shape for this flower. To borrow a New World Order word, there needs to be some **restructuring** around here. These beaks of ours need gradual adaptation. Strain, strain, strain, bend, bend, bend, curve, curve, curve", said the bird.

Initially, there was no change and the birds who just could not get their beaks into those flowers gradually passed away. Fortunately however, just before each generation died, in spite of their lack of sustenance and good nutrition, the majority of them managed to mate, thus keeping the species going.

Although we cannot explain how, each generation managed to stay alive, and wouldn't you believe it, **after only 500,000 years**, one morning, one of these birds woke up with his now perfected morning cry, "Strain, strain, strain, bend, bend, bend, curve, curve, curve, you wretched beak". All at once, he gave a glad cry. It was starting to happen. A slight curve in the right direction and not only that, a slight lengthening had also taken place....etc etc.

I personally have no objection to any person putting their faith in this type of scenario. It is such fun that I am considering writing a humorous childrens' book on the subject.

Now, we move on to stage 2 of our belief system. Scientist Lovelock now tells us that there is a "**regulator**". Could it be that he is the type of scientist that knows, without the aid of a double blind test, that 1+1=2. This looked promising until he called the "regulator" Gaia.

As we said before, if there is no devil, then who is doing his work? Who is it that allows people to take the giant step from "nothing evolved into a world of design" to a regulator evolved (or created) a world of design and then called the regulator after a character from a Greek myth. Gaia! Who on earth is Gaia? A mythological character!

We are almost as badly off as we were before.

Fact - Everybody believes in God - We all cry out for help either audibly or silently when we are in trouble. This is just as well, I guess, as the Lord, in His mercy, allows some to sneak through at the very last minute.

I had an uncle who lay dying in New Zealand hospital. Having paid him a last visit, I stood in the doorway and called back, "Uncle Frank, I may never see you again. Please remember God's promise. *"Whosoever shall call upon the Name of the Lord shall be saved."*[8]

Did he call? I won't know until I reach my final destination.

A Clear Statement

When all the whitewashing is over, the mouth speaking clap-trap and mens' opinions are silenced forever, the day when every knee bows and every tongue confesses that Jesus Christ is Lord, then men will unitedly understand the purpose for our existence. Not to spend our days as religious bores, but to live out our lives in humble relationship with Almighty God and His Son, the Lord Jesus Christ.

It is written *"And for Thy pleasure, they are and were created"*[9].

In the meantime, our New World Order planners will pass bills to make all religions valid, even though they will condemn men who trust in them to the everlasting fires of Hell.

Laugh if you will. **I challenge you to close the book at this point and not open it again**. Who was it that said, *"And fear not them which kill the body, but are not able to kill the soul, but rather fear him which is able to destroy both soul and body in Hell."*[10]

Religious issues are so much part of some peoples' make-up that they will kill for it, or involve themselves in social action, particularly as they become older.

These dear ones ignore the true plan of God for us - **a relationship** so strong that a selfish, ignorant, self-serving hypocrite can, by God's grace and power, become a humble, sacrificial servant of God. This happens miraculously as one comes to the cross of Christ as a sinner, leaves his sin there, and arises to new life.

For this prayer of commitment, please turn to the back of this book now!

Media - Prediction - what people learn and know about current events.

Fulfilment - Not many are aware of the fact that certain individuals have been appointed to **vet the news**.

They are appointed by those who are setting up the New World Order. I have on my desk a copy of an audio tape, recorded at the World Environmental Conference, held in Denver, Colorado.

Present at that conference were representatives of major corporations, Rockefeller, Rothschilds, Maurice Strong, and most importantly, an American friend of ours, George Hunt from Boulder, Colorado, who was investigating this world government data.

As sure as I sit here writing this article, I have now heard this arrogant statement, spoken by one of the leaders at this important conference.

"We must keep this information from the cannon-fodder that unfortunately populate the earth."

That's you and me!

Unfortunately for these rascals, books like this one are bringing enlightenment to those who read them. Access to the truth is still available however and it is most exciting! The words of this passage are very true - *"If any man lack wisdom, let him ask of God who giveth liberally to all men and upbraideth not."*[11] End quote.

Continuity - Prediction - the power to appoint who follows in your footsteps.

Fulfilment - I have in my possession a tape of an interview with an ex-Prime Minister of New Zealand being interviewed over a New Zealand radio station.

'Top of the Morning', 20th December 1997 - (D.......d L......e interviewed by B.....n E......s). This was the man who was apparently in charge of the Labour Party of this country, when the test case was applied.

The key dates - 1984 - new budget.

- 1987 - the implementation of the IMF wrecking plan.

Remember again the words of Barber Conable, the President of the World Bank who visited the guinea pig country of New Zealand in the late 1980's.

"New Zealand's economic restructuring was a role model for other countries which also had to adjust their policies to achieve growth." (Break quote - see pages 135-136 'Final Notice - It is my personal opinion that this man was telling the truth in the course of this interview.)

Continue quote - *"Q. When you were elected in 1984, did you know what you were going to do?*

A. No."

Author's note - It is therefore clear that although New Zealand borrowed the **loans** from the IMF during the year 1961, the **conditions** were not revealed to this man and his four implementers until after they were elected to power. Thus, there was **no secret agenda**. **It was not a New Zealand designed plan as we have already made clear. Remember the think tanks? The Adam Smith Institute, The Mont Pelerin Society and the Business Round Table....**

Continue quote - *"Ex.P.M. - "We implemented policies we did not recognise. Traditional Labour voters felt they had been betrayed."*

Author's note - To any sceptics I say, "This man is agreeing with what we say about governmental power and authority - there is none!

Continue quote - *"Ex.P.M. - "Politicians can do a rain-dance around what is happening but they are powerless to do anything about it. You could run a cabinet today with about 5 people."* End quote.

Author's note - The interview continued on and our ex-P.M. revealed that **the Prime Minister was not the conductor of an orchestra, but merely a player of a long-playing record.**

There it is - **continuity**.

When asked by the interviewer if it was **the machine** that had the power, the Ex.P.M. answered - *"The machine does not allow any person to have power. The power lies with an elite class of people. The individual has no real power."* End quote.

The reader, having digested these remarks may even begin to feel some real sadness for these politicians who happened to be in the wrong job at the wrong time.

The elite he referred to of course, were members of the groups George Bush referred to as '1000 Points of Light'. In New Zealand, the Business Round Table and the IMF had a lot to say during these days.

When asked about our new political system entitled **MMP - Mixed Member Proportional**, he replied in part, *"A zoo. A talking shop of madness...."* End quote.

Author's note - A very perceptive and apt description.

No Other Options

Thus we see the Labour treasurer of the day was ultimately **ousted** as he implemented the IMF conditions. The next treasurer, a woman in the National party was also **ousted**, as she was forced to continue the plan.

The next treasurer under MMP is also obviously struggling against his better nature, to continue on with the plan. His original policies seem to have miraculously **changed**.

Continuity is essential! As Fabius said "Otherwise all your waiting has been in vain."

Apparent Political Suicide

Watch the news carefully from now on and observe the casualty list of Presidents, Prime Ministers and Treasurers. These will all incur the wrath of angry voters as they implement the IMF policies and conditions. Take Australia as a good example with their politics in chaos, halfway through the year 1998. The One Nation political party has been formed by persons trying to bypass the overseas think tanks' influence on politics.

Their policies can only be mooted however, whilst they are in opposition, for should they ever be included in a government coalition, or similar, they would find, to their dismay, that under the New World Order plans, one is no longer allowed to think for one's self. Everything is decided by the think tanks, and encouraged by the Business Council of Australia.

In New Zealand, the Business Round Table plays this role.

Rule

Governments must now do what they are told or the investors sprout wings and fly elsewhere!

Ultimately however, all is bright on the horizon for some of these government puppets, as the New World Order can upgrade them quietly to other positions of power, if it is deemed necessary.

Footnotes

1   John 3:3
2   Galatians 6:7
3   James 5:1
4   James 5:4
5   Proverbs 22:15
6   Proverbs 29:15
7   Revelation 22:15
8   Acts 2:21
9   Revelation 4:11
10 Matthew 10:28
11 James 1:5

CHAPTER SEVENTEEN

AMERICA AND FREEMASONRY

I'm sorry I have to keep harping on and on about Freemasonry but what you are about to read is absolutely shocking, yet sadly, it is all true.

Along with the vast majority of this world's citizens, I always believed that the USA was the **home of the brave and the land of the free**.

Are you sometimes tempted to wish you have never learned certain information? Too late! Once you read it or hear it, it is yours for life.

Precis

In our fifth book, "Better Than Nostradamus", we outline very clearly and carefully, the history of the two seals on the reverse side of every US$1 bill. We learned also that the top Freemasons have a **dualistic concept** on life, meaning that in a perfect world, everything will have an opposite i.e. male - female, light - dark, good - evil.

Albert Pike and other leading Masons carry through with this argument and add Lucifer as the opposite to Adonay. Then, evil upon evil, they reverse the roles and call Lucifer, light and goodness, and Adonay, darkness and evil.

Two groups settled America.

A. **The Pilgrim Fathers** - their aim was religious freedom.
B. **Freemasons and occultists** - their aim was to place Lucifer on the throne of the world.

Q. How do I know?
A. A chance encounter one night in Seattle, Washington State, U.S.A., led us to a friend's house. There we met a young lady with a very large and interesting book under her arm. It was entitled "The Secret Teachings of all Ages" by Manly P. Hall, a top Masonic writer. Supposing that the book might contain some added information that would provide some more pieces to the jigsaw puzzle, I subsequently paid her $US20 then went off with the book and I trust she went off to purchase another one.

I will guarantee that 99.9% of my book's readers do not have Mr Hall's book in their library. Its contents are **blatantly outrageous** as he tells us in very clear language, the aims of the Freemasons and other occultists who settled the country of America.

ANNOUNCING THE BIRTH OF THE NEW WORLD ORDER (WITHOUT GOD), UNDER THE ALL-SEEING EYE OF SATAN, THE ANTI-CHRIST, 666

By the way, if you can find a copy, go for it. Have your mind boggled as mine has been, trying to read and absorb even some of the material there presented. Friends that I have shown it to reel in disbelief at the masses of **occult knowledge** that most people have no idea exists. The word to describe it is **incredible**.

I hurriedly flicked through its pages searching for information about America and the seals on the reverse side of their $US1 bill. Reader, I implore you - do not think evil of this author - **please do not shoot the messenger!**

Read and Understand the Message

P.XC and P.XCI.

"European mysticism was not dead at the time the United States of America was founded. The hand of the Mysteries controlled in the establishment of the new government, for the signature of the Mysteries may still be seen on the Great Seal of the United States of America.

Careful analysis of the seal discloses a mass of occult and Masonic symbols, chief among them, the so-called American eagle....only the student of symbolism can see through the subterfuge and realise that the American eagle upon the Great Seal is but a conventionalised phoenix." Break quote.

Author's note - what is a phoenix? Webster's New World Dictionary says - *"Egyptian myth - a bird which lived for 500 years and then consumed itself in fire, rising renewed from the ashes."*

Meaning

a) Man's first attempt to set up a One World Government was the Tower of Babel. The Lord in His wisdom, saw that if all mankind got together in this manner, and pooled all their knowledge and expertise, it would ultimately destroy them.

Therefore, He put a stop to it.

b) The evil power behind mankind was not so easily subdued. The phoenix is rising again in your life-time.

- It is evil.
- It is deceptive.
- It is based on lies.
- It is supernatural.
- It is all-embracing.
- It is based on surveillance.

- It will have total control.
- Dissidents will be done away with.

George Bush called it the New World Order. Jimmy Carter called the plan Global 2000 - meaning that by the end of the year 2000, the IMF loans - conditions - selling out of sovereignty scam would have affected all nations in some way.

Every country in the world will then be brought under the all-seeing eye umbrella found on the reverse side of every US$1 bill.

This will be called the **Global Village.** (It's theme song will probably be something along the lines of "**We are the world**".)

Now you may ask where does America fit into all of this?

We now continue our brief, yet revealing, quote from Manly P. Hall's book - "The Secret Teachings of All Ages" P.XCI.

*"Not only were many of the founders of the United States' Government Masons, but they **received aid** from a secret and august body existing in **Europe** which helped them to establish this country **for a peculiar and particular purpose** known only to the **initiated few**.*

*The Great Seal is the signature of this exalted body - unseen and for the most part, unknown and the unfinished pyramid upon its reverse side is a trestleboard, setting forth symbolically **the task** to the accomplishment of which the United States Government was dedicated from the day of its inception."* End quote.

2 Questions

a) **Who are the initiated few?**
b) **What was the task?**

If we can find the answer to these missing jigsaw pieces, believe me, it will make a great deal of difference to the way you view the media reports on America.

At the risk of repeating myself, we have outlined in our fifth book, 'Better Than Nostradamus', the identity of the **initiated few**.

In Freemasonry, which has links with the super-secret Illuminati, according to the Encyclopaedia Britannica, Vol.12, 1963 *"Those men who understand the mysteries of Egypt, Babylon and witch-craft, along with their mystical writings found in the Kabalah. **These are the initiated few** - The **Elect**, The **Adepts** and the **Sages**."* End quote.

Further Light on the Subject for Doubters

On the same page in Manly Hall's book we read, *"If anyone **doubts** the*

presence of Masonic and occult influences at the time the Great Seal was designed, he should give due consideration to the comments of Professor Charles Eliot Norton of Harvard, who wrote concerning the unfinished pyramid and the All-Seeing Eye, which adorned the reverse of the seal as follows - "The device adopted by Congress is practically incapable of effective treatment, it can hardly (however artistically treated by the designer) look otherwise than a **dull emblem of the Masonic fraternity**.*""*
(The History of the Seal of the United States.) End quote.

The Kabalah

An ancient occult book written by occultists in the town of Zefat, situated on the mountain above the Sea of Galilee in Israel. This book is used by top Masons, witches, and some religious Jews.

Read now what Albert Pike, a 33rd degree Freemason says about the Kabalah in his book "Morals and Dogma", page 744 - *"...all the Masonic associations owe to it their Secrets and their Symbols.*

The Kabalah alone consecrates the alliance of the Universal Reason and the Divine Word, it establishes by the counterpoises of two forces apparently opposite, **the eternal balance of being**, *it alone reconciles Reason with Faith, Power with Liberty, Science with Mystery, it has the keys of the Present, the Past and the Future..."* End quote.

Author's note - This is simply the Eastern notion of dualism. In their eyes, everything has an opposite. Sad really, because Almighty God does not have an opposite! *"God is light and in Him is no darkness at all."*[1]

Of course, Freemasons, basing their beliefs on this ancient occultist book, damn themselves by agreeing that Lucifer (Satan) is the opposite to the true God of Israel i.e. Adonay.

They audaciously reverse the roles. **Adonay becomes the bad guy and Lucifer becomes the good guy.**

Lucifer is represented on the reverse side of the U.S.$1 bill as the eye in the triangle. We are positive in our identification as he is setting up a **Novus Ordo Seclorum** - a heathenistic, ungodly, Godless, **secular** one world government.

We have adequately answered question a) and now for question b) What was the task?

Answer - To place Lucifer on the throne of the world.

That gave you a shock didn't it?

1. Therefore, the task set before the United States government is known

only to the top Illuminati men and their friends, plus a few others, such as this book's author, and now you, the reader.

2. This task is to bring in a devilish one world government with God's enemy seated on the throne.

It sounds weird when you first hear it, yet upon a little further thought, it makes sense - for example:

- The murder of President Kennedy - a lying cover up.
- The murder of U.S. citizens at Waco, Texas - a lying cover up.
- The murder in Oklahoma - a lying cover up.
- The death of Ron Brown - plane crash or gunshot wound to the head?
- The death of Vince Foster - suicide or murder?
- The Reagan administration leaving hostages in Iran awaiting the U.S. election.
- The Clinton shenanigans.
- The cover up of the AIDS cure - Polyatomic Oxygen Therapy (ozone) - See the Internet.

Not much intelligence is needed to know that something is wrong here.

Illustration: There is a man in court being cross-examined on a murder charge.

"Your honour, there I was on the corner of the street, leaning up against a telephone pole, cleaning my fingernails with my pocket knife.

Then, your honour, this gentleman suddenly appeared from around the corner, walking backwards, and ran into my knife - **32 times**...."

As I travel, I tend to be on the lookout for interesting and relevant material. Look at this - 'Daily Telegraph', Great Britain, 18th December 1997 - *"Clinton pressed to hold Brown murder enquiry.*

A number of black leaders are urging President Clinton to investigate evidence that Ron Brown, found dead after a plane crash last year, may have been murdered.

...wants him to follow up pathologist's claims that a "wound to the secretary's head may have been caused by a gunshot.

...suspicion of foul play can no longer be dismissed as a conspiracy theory held only by cranks, eager to tarnish the President.

*Chris Ruddy, an investigative journalist who made his name **amassing evidence of foul play** in the 1993 "suicide" of Vince Foster, deputy counsel at the White House, has produced photographs that appear to show a 45 calibre bullet hole in the top of Mr Brown's head.*

Mr Ruddy also quoted Lt. Col. Steve Cogswell, a medical examiner at the Armed Forces Institute of Pathology, of saying of the accident investigation, "the whole thing stinks".

*...Mr Brown was one of 35 people who died aboard the military jet when it crashed during a trade mission to Croatia. **At the time, he was being investigated for corruption by the Justice Department and documents about his finances were allegedly shredded after his death."***
Break quote.

Author's note - This is in the '**land of the free**' and '**the home of the brave**'. Mr Brown is now free of his corruption charges. He was a brave man to be flying at all, with those type of friends in the White House.

Continue quote - *"No object found in the crash wreckage was the right size to have made a hole in Mr Brown's head.*

Photographs of the x-rays (the originals have been lost), show what could be a "lead snowstorm" in the brain, consistent with a bullet disintegrating..." End quote.

Author's note - It is also of very significant interest, I remember reading at the time, that **the plane was not carrying a black box flight recorder.** Why not?

The Evil Power Over America

Let us now identify the ruling demonic spirit that rules over this so-called mighty country. It is revealed to us by the eye in the triangle on the reverse side of every US$1 bill.

Originally, the eye of Horus in Egyptian mythology, this all-seeing eye principle is the basis for the surveillance of every member of society who lives in the confines of a Global Village.

Cameras are being installed everywhere, purportedly to cut back on crime, but in actuality, it is the foundation of the eye of Big Brother. Adam Weishaupt, the founder of the Illuminati, called this eye - **The Insinuating Brethren**.

The triangle has its explanation in our book 'Better Than Nostradamus'. It stands for the highly-secret Masonic degree which is just below the Illuminati. This degree has as its name, **the Palladium**, or Cult of the Triangles - **Lucifer, or Satan, the king-pin of evil.**

As other spiritual forces rule over the affairs of each country, each spirit may be identified by the strong negative traits of that particular nation. Thus, we can now state authoritatively the identity of the negative spirit guiding the affairs of the United States of America.

Notice that the triangle on the US$1 bill is radiated. There is a glow coming from it. I am quoting from the Encyclopaedia of Freemasonry, page 946, by Albert G. Mackey.

"....the true Masonic idea of this glory is that it symbolises that Eternal Light of Wisdom which surrounds the Supreme Architect as a sea of glory, and from him as a common centre emanates to the universe of his creation..." End quote.

Author's note - The Freemasons themselves, in the upper degrees, know exactly who this Supreme Architect is - Lucifer (Satan), the Devil himself.

It is true that before his fall, through his pride and his beauty he was full of beauty and wisdom, but it was later said of him through the prophet, *"Thou has corrupted thy wisdom by reason of thy brightness; I will cast thee to the ground; I will lay thee before kings; that they may behold thee."*[2] End quote.

Let me assure you - there is only one true living God and His Name is not Lucifer! This guy is a usurping imposter! **Mr Freemason, shake your head and wake up - you've been conned!**

Lucifer - The Capstone Needs to be Placed on the Pyramid

This being the case, the Ayatollah Khomeini unwittingly had it correct, when he referred to America as *the great Satan*.

Read herewith a verification of this latest statement. Albert Pike again in his book, "Morals and Dogma", page 321.

*"**Lucifer** the light-bearer. Strange and mysterious name to give to the Spirit of Darkness! **Lucifer**, the Son of the Morning. It is **he** who bears the **light** and with its splendour, intolerable, blinds feeble, sensual or selfish souls! **Doubt it not**."* End quote.

America is run by the Devil

For the time being - this is correct. **The task that has been set for this country is the takeover of every other country on earth. To steal their independence, and sovereignty, and ultimately unite them in a Global Village under the leadership of one man in particular.**

This man's title is **Antichrist**.

This piece of information may cause you to wish to close this book and forget it. My advice is that you don't! Just continue reading.

Freemasonry's Influence on America

On page 68 of our book "Better Than Nostradamus", we see a map of Washington D.C. When I show this map via an overhead projector in our public meetings, there is always a gasp from the audience.

Built into the streets of that very important city are the symbols of the compass and square and the satanic five pointed inverted pentagram.

A. One end of the compass stops directly at the white House.

B. The single point of the five pointed pentagram also stops at the White House. Therefore the incumbent President has a satanic force hitting him from two directions.

Now can you see why the world sniggers at the obvious corruption connected with the Presidents of the United States of America e.g. President Nixon - Watergate scandal, President Reagan - Arms for hostages scandal, President Clinton - Not enough room in this book for all the scandals attributed to this man!

'Charisma' magazine, November 1997, printed out an interesting article on Freemasonry. We quote in part the article on Washington D.C.

"The Residence Act of July 16, 1790, authorised the President to appoint 3 commissioners who were to survey the land and mark out the borders of the district. It was to be exactly 10 miles square.

Then, in April 1791, **members of local Masonic lodges gathered** *at Jones' Point, Alexandria, Virginia,* **to lay the cornerstone** *of the federal district* **according to Masonic ritual** *- which included consecrating it with corn, wine and oil.*

...through Masonic rituals, **our nation's government has been symbolically offered to the kingdom of darkness."** End quote.

And That's Not All

Taken from the same magazine, we read - *"President George Washington commissioned Pierre Charles L'Enfant, a Mason, to design the U.S. federal district. The Capitol, White House and nearby memorials, which were added over the years, became part of an intricate Masonic design that includes the ancient Egyptian obelisk - the Washington monument serving as its central focus. Some say the total design represents a casket positioned according to Masonic burial specifications."* End quote.

Freemasons - Declare Yourselves!

There are five books that precede this one. Each of these books has a section on Freemasonry. "Why", you may ask.

It is connected with the highly secret Illuminati, One World Government, conspirators. These men are setting up a **satanic One World Government** and by way of proof of this statement, look at the two strange seals on the reverse side of every US$1 bill.

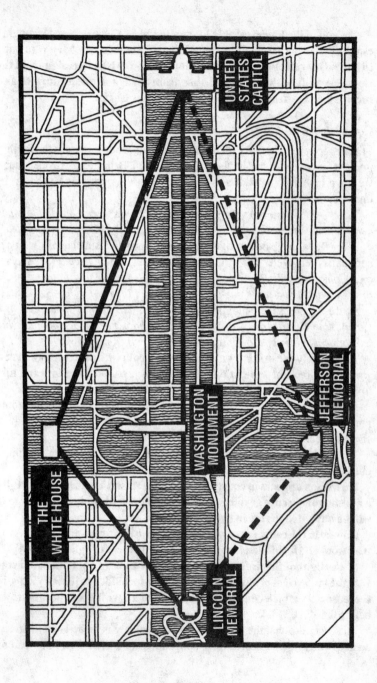

UNITED STATES CAPITOL

THE WHITE HOUSE

WASHINGTON MONUMENT

JEFFERSON MEMORIAL

LINCOLN MEMORIAL

The god of the Freemasons is Lucifer (Satan). This has been thoroughly established in our last book - "Better Than Nostradamus". **Men who hope to enter Heaven one day, are therefore, well-advised to resign from the Lodge, renounce the oaths and obligations you took upon yourself, and receive God's offer of salvation through Jesus Christ**.

Corruption of the Law

In every country where they have a Freemason's lodge, there is the **facility present** for **corruption of the law**. On page 51 of "Better Than Nostradamus", we have revealed the oath as sworn by a North American Mason in the third degree.

Viz - *"I will keep a worthy brother Master Mason's secrets inviolable, when communicated to or received by me as such, murder and treason excepted."*

In the Royal Arch degree of the York Rite, even that small qualification is summarily removed. The candidate swears that *"I will keep all the secrets of a Companion Royal Arch Mason (when communicated to me as such, or I knowing them to be such), without exceptions."*

At this degree, the candidate also swears, *"I will not speak evil of a Companion Royal Arch Mason, behind his back nor before his face, but will appraise him of all approaching danger, if in my power."*

This simply means that an officer of the court who knew of an arrest warrant taken out against a brother Mason, would have to warn him immediately so he could flee the jurisdiction.

A Mason who was told of a brother Mason's crimes, even including rape, robbery, or child abuse, would have to keep his knowledge of these crimes a secret, even in a court of law!

A Royal Arch Mason who knew of a Companion Mason's being a murderer or a traitor, would have to keep his knowledge a secret.

If a Mason appears in court against a non-Mason, all he has to do is give a number of obscure gestures or words to a Masonic judge, and this man will be obligated to rule in his favour.

No-one in the court room will be any the wiser (except another Mason), who would be forbidden from bringing the incident to light.

In the light of this information, it is clear that any person connected with the law system of any country should be forbidden to join any lodge or secret society which could in any way interfere with his duties. (Written before the 30.10.96).

It is clear also that the corruption of national law is made possible in any country where Masons take their obligations seriously. Therefore, careful note must be taken in future, of any strange decisions made in matters of law.

We in New Zealand will possibly need to start the ball rolling, by starting our investigations at the southern end of the South Island. There are many citizens who are now crying "Enough is enough".

Hooray. The Cat is Out of the Bag!

'Daily Telegraph', Sydney, 19th February 1998 - *"Brits will out Freemasons.*

British Freemasons were in shock yesterday *after the Government said all new recruits to the police and judiciary must declare publicly their membership in the society whose very existence is based on secrecy.*

It is the first time a government has taken such a radical measure in the history of Freemasonry, according to experts. ***There are an estimated one million Freemasons in Britain.***

The new rules will apply to police, probation and prison services, as well as magistrates, judges and crown prosecutors, Home Secretary,.......said. Their names will be put on a register." End quote.

The 'Times' of London, 20th February 1998, has the following headline. *"Masons face showdown with MP's."* End quote.

The front page of the 'Financial Times', 20th February 1998 - *"Freemasons defy MP's in clash over secrecy."* End quote.

The 'Express', 20th February 1998 headlines in massive print, scream out the following - *"**MP'S MAY JAIL TOP MASON**. He refuses to name police"*, and in a further article, *"Mason defies prison threat".*

Now you can see how these poor men allowed themselves to be duped into a trap. **Because they are bound through their weird system of morality to fulfil their Freemason's obligations, they cannot obey the law of their country.**

It's about time all this was brought out for public scrutiny.

Of course, readers who are familiar with our publications are aware that some of the folk involved in the upper degrees of masonry have a **secret agenda** for the setting up of **a One World Government by the year 2000**.

Unfortunately, although their aims in some cases seem to make sense, the prophecies tell us that ultimately, every citizen of the world will be under the iron heel of a monster, of an even more depraved nature than Adolf Hitler.

His title - **Antichrist.**

Laugh now - repent at your leisure!

FOOTNOTES

[1]   1 John 1:5
[2]   Ezekiel 28:17

CHAPTER EIGHTEEN

AMERICA YOU ARE DOOMED AND YOU'RE SO YOUNG TOO!

All intelligent people believe in God.

They work on the old principle that **nothing begets nothing.**

Therefore, **if there is no God, we are not here**! Don't you agree?

Years ago, when we were youngsters, we were involved in a Christian Open Air service. A man strolled up to our platform and made his arresting statement - "There is no God!"

My friend, David McBride, the speaker at the time, answered him in this manner. "Did it ever occur to you sir, that because you do not have the ability to be everywhere at once, God may be somewhere where you are not. Therefore, in claiming as you do, that there is no God, you yourself are claiming to be God, as you would need to be everywhere at once yourself to make such an authoritative statement."

Any person, therefore, who does not believe that there is a God, cannot possibly be really reading this book as you are not really here. Please lay it down immediately and stop fooling yourself.

Q. Will Almighty God allow the United States of America, with the occult, witchcraft signs on their dollar bill, continue on in their evil ways?

A. Certainly not! Remember, America was founded by the Masons for a peculiar and particular purpose. **Following the computer collapse at midnight, 31st December 1999, the Plan will begin to unfold.**

The Gulf War Syndrome

How is it that so many of the Gulf War Veterans are suffering from this weird illness? Who gave it to them?

The answer is, **their own government did!** Is there no end to the evil these people are capable of?

Christchurch 'Press', 24th December 1997 - *"U.S. Soldiers given an Unlicensed Vaccine.*

The Pentagon has admitted that a vaccine with unknown health effects was given to 8000 United States' soldiers in the Gulf War, but said the injections were optional in at least some cases." Break quote.

Author's note - In my opinion, it would have made better reading if this last portion had not been included. It is clear that the Pentagon is guilty of malpractice and that possibly two or three soldiers were told they didn't need to submit to this vaccination. If there was not a **good scare story told at the time**, about possible chemical attacks, just ask yourself, would you accept a vaccination if it didn't seem necessary?

Continue quote - *"The comments came in response to a story in a Cleveland newspaper about injections of **botulinum toxoid vaccine** which was meant to protect against chemical and biological warfare.*

*The vaccine is now being studied as a possible source of the health problem associated with **"Gulf War Syndrome"**.* Break quote.

Author's note - Some time ago, we viewed a video clip where one U.S. Army female doctor was threatened with imprisonment if she did not administer this dangerous vaccine. She said "It is not ethical for me to give this to our boys, without knowing its long-term effects."

Continue quote - *"While the military had permission from the **U.S. Food and Drug Administration** to give the vaccine **without consent** of the soldiers, the U.S. Central Command decided to make the programme optional, Defence Department spokesman.....said.*

However, Mr.... said he was not sure which soldiers had been told about the injection.

He said it was possible not all the troops were given a choice to reject it." Break quote.

Author's note - **The Federal Drug Administration (FDA) generally will only pass a drug or a substance as being suitable for human application after conducting copious tests. However, in this case, they passed an untested substance as being suitable for human application. We must now ask the question 'why?'**

Not only that, the Defence Department spokesman passes a few pitifully inadequate remarks to try and get his people off the hook. They are all highly embarrassed because somebody found them out. But that's not all - read on!

Please notice the words "**without consent**". What a murderous plan!

Continue quote - *"A transcript of an army ethics committee's meeting in **Maryland** on October 4ᵗʰ, 1990, showed that army physicians were not confident the **unlicensed vaccine** would protect troops from illness..."* End quote.

Author's note - As soon as I read the name **Maryland**, I smelt the proverbial rat! Turning quickly to Page 115 of our third book, 'Final Notice', I saw that it was the chapter on AIDS and its possible origins.

A Dr Theodore Strecker talks about the NCI Laboratories at **Fort Detrick, Maryland**, being involved in the creation of strange viruses. He says the AIDS virus was engineered in these laboratories by virologists. **It couldn't engineer itself**.

Q. To whom are these people responsible? 8000 soldiers used as guinea-pigs with the blessing of the FDA. Absolutely shocking!

For further information, please write to American Gulf War Veterans' Association, 3506 Highway South 117, Sugarland, Texas, 77478-4401, U.S.A. Ph. toll-free - 1-800-23-7631. This video will provoke extreme anger as you learn of the lies and deceit surrounding this cover up.

A Clear Prophecy

On page 146-147 of our fifth book, 'Better Than Nostradamus', we record 25 reasons why the city of New York is in for a very difficult time very shortly. (Date of prediction was the 10th February 1998.) New York is the centre of world banking, the home of the Illuminati, and the United Nations.

Here is the prophecy given in 96 A.D. which will find its fulfilment in the near future.

The prophecy comes in two parts.

A. Sudden death and mourning, then

B. The cleaning up process involving fire

Prophecy

A. Therefore shall her **plagues** come in one day, death and mourning and famine

B. And she shall be utterly burned with fire

C. For strong is the Lord God who judgeth her

'Sunday Telegraph', U.K., 15th September 1997 - *"Fears Grow of Germ Warfare in U.S.*

*Saddam Hussein has a stock of **anthrax, botulin, and other agents of germ warfare** that could be released with deadly effect in any major city in **Britain or the United States**.*

...You could spray biological agents from crop-dusters, you could even drive around Washington with the stuff coming out of the exhaust of a car, and it would kill tens of thousands of people said Dr....a former lecturer at the U.S. Naval War College, and now a fellow at the Foreign Policy Research Institute of Philadelphia.

...Iraq has....defied the United Nations' Special Commission by refusing to hand over any of its biological weapons.

The U.S. Ambassador to the United Nations, ..., has warned that

Saddam Hussein has enough "anthrax" to kill every man, woman and child in the world.

...the loudest cries of alarm have been coming from outside the government. A small but growing group of experts in Washington has begun to suspect that **Iraq** could be the real force behind the wave of **terrorist attacks** that has traumatised America in the 1990's.

...there is even some suspicion that Iraq could have had a hand in the bombing of the Murrah Federal Building in Oklahoma City on April 19th, 1995.

The defence team of the leading suspect, Timothy McVeigh, has been travelling extensively in the Middle East and the Philippines.

...last month, the FBI announced that it was transferring 500 agents to beef up its counter-terrorism capability. **The move came just weeks after the crash of TWA flight 800 off New York on July 17th."** End quote.

Author's note - Another cover-up! Masses of witnesses observed a missile streaking up towards the aircraft. Is there no end to the U.S. authorities' lies and deception?

Continue quote - "...Increasingly, the question being asked in Washington every time a bomb goes off is which of the pariah states is guilty - Iran or Iraq? And when will it strike next?" End quote.

Author's note - Someone reads this material and judges too quickly. Just a moment - you have heard of the 'Time' magazine, haven't you? They agree with the author of this book.

'Time' magazine, 1st December 1997 - "**America the Vulnerable**.

Saddam Hussein's unwatched arsenal of poisons and germs can redouble the threat to America, and the terrorists are already among us.

...In other words, yes they are in danger. Americans no longer believe that their country is immune to terrorism as they did for decades and they are spending big money to fight the threat - more than $400 million in federal counterterror programs alone.

...**experts insist the U.S. is essentially insecure. The borders are porous**, the government cannot keep track of routine visa violators, and the population is forever on the move. The U.S. is a sea into which evildoers can dive and remain submerged.

Terrorists, like anyone else, have little difficulty obtaining guns or the simple makings for oil-barrel truck bombs.

Now the new terror could be an even more lethal destroyer-microbes. Germ weapons are small, cheap, easy to hide, simple to dispense and horribly effective. They may be the treat of the near future.

Officials in Washington are deeply worried about what some of them call "strategic crime".

*It wouldn't take much. **A gram of anthrax culture contains a trillion spores**, theoretically enough for 100 million fatal doses. The stuff can be spread into the air with backpack sprayers or even perfume atomisers. The U.N.'s specialists say that 45 kg of anthrax bacteria sprayed around a city of 1 million could kill 36,000 people within a week. And Saddam has produced anthrax in large amounts, along with botulinum, a poison that kills by paralysing the victim and aflatoxin, a carcinogen.*

*...**Saddam would hardly produce such weapons if he never intended to use them.** And when might he unleash them? **He would want to take as many enemies with him as he could,** the agency predicted.*

*...**New York City was getting with the program last week, trying to face up to the danger.** The city has spent millions for training and equipment since the World Trade Center bombing, much of it provided by the Defence Department...Even so, some experts are unimpressed. "The New York region", says.....former head of security for El Al, the Israeli airline, "is no better prepared for a terrorist attack today than it was before the World Trade Centre bombing"....... "* End quote.

In the same month, the 'Time' magazine quoted Louis Farrakhan, U.S. leader of the Nation of Islam speaking in Tehran. *"You can quote me. God will destroy America at the hands of the Muslims."* End quote.

What a nice man. And to think the Americans still allow this gentleman to live on their soil.

'Weekly Telegraph', 6th May 1997 - *"President Clinton has scored a major foreign policy victory with the U.S. Senate's ratification of a treaty outlawing the manufacture, storage and use of a long list of chemical weapons.*

The Chemical Weapons Convention, passed by 74 votes to 26, also calls for existing stocks to be destroyed by 2007.

Under the convention, the U.S. is obliged to disclose in detail its defences, equipment and techniques for countering a chemical attack to fellow signatories.

*Iran arguably the U.S.'s deadliest enemy has ratified the treaty, **Iraq** and even North Korea **could** soon sign."* End quote.

Author's note - I'll bet Saddam loves this treaty.

By now, you may clearly see the reason for America not coming to the assistance of Israel at this moment of crisis. There is an imminent threat for Israel as they await the long predicted threat of invasion by Russia, Iran, Libya, Turkey, Germany and others. Prophesied approximately 593 B.C.

CHAPTER NINETEEN

BRITANNIA RULES THE WAVES

Or so the words of the old song tells us!

It's simply not so you know. Great Britain, as it has been known for many years now, is finished - all washed up. The catch-words used in this case are **Devolution in Great Britain**.

So new is the word devolution that is it is not even listed in Webster's new World Dictionary. It simply means that both Scotland and Wales have decided to go their own ways and run their own affairs. This also means that poor England has been left out in the cold by herself.

It is not without significance that all around the world today, many of the ethnic groups within certain countries are striving for independence. As the prophecies tell us, that at a certain time in history.

"Ethnos Will Fight Against Ethnos" (Ethnic versus ethnic)

Great Britain it appears is no longer the odd man out, or the exception to the rule. Already, **Scotland** has voted for a separate form of government as also has **Wales**.

Please take careful note of the following media article.

'Sunday Telegraph', 14th September 1997 - *"Scots vote accords with Brussels master plan.*

There was even more rejoicing in Brussels than in Glasgow over Scotland's devolution vote...

*Both Scotland and Wales are already ear-marked on commission maps as Euro-regions, while England is broken up into 8 regions, Northern, North-Eastern, and North-Western, East and West Midlands, East Anglia, South East and South West. The next step in the **master plan** after Wales votes for its assembly will be unveiled in the Autumn...*

The intention is that these will build up their own direct relationship with Brussels,** fuelled by lavish handouts given direct to each region (**indeed, the regions already have offices in Brussels for this purpose.**) In due course, these will also be given elected assemblies, and **the breakup of the United Kingdom will be almost complete.

*The idea is that the more Europe can be split up in this way the more obvious will become the need to **run centrally** those services which the new regions are too small to run on their own - **common defence and*** *security forces, a common judicial (law) system, and the rest, not forgetting that common currency.*

Of course, when one puts all this in a newspaper, one risks being accused of paranoid xenophobia, but then the vocabulary of abuse of our Europhile friends, when one catches them out in what they are really up to, has always been strangely limited..." End quote.

Author's note - there is no doubt that this breakup of Great Britain will also extend to squabbling over lakes, rivers and boundaries etc, and whilst this is going on, the World Government people will further their plans in the taking over of the independence and sovereignty of every country on earth.

Prime Minister, Tony Blair, and Iraq

Let me state at the very outset, I like Tony Blair. In a world of obviously unqualified, and in many cases, unsuitable leadership, it is a joy to see an enthusiastic, smiling face whenever he appears on T.V.

By now it is clear that all politicians world-wide are only just now beginning to realise that theirs is a very precarious job.

Obey U.N. charters and the dictates of such groups as the OECD along with your national big business advisors and you remain in your position. Try and run the country your way and you are down the road immediately.

Before that last British election, we read in the British press - *"Blair immortalised.*

Britain's opposition leader, Tony Blair, is to be immortalised as a rough, tough, comic strip character who never loses his trademark toothy grin, according to the Daily Telegraph. The newspaper said the Labour leader, odds on with British bookies to win the next general election, is to star in a one-off strip in the 20th anniversary issue of 2000 A.D., whose biggest star is the violent Judge Dredd." End quote.

Hello, hello, hello, Tony has been to New Zealand

It is for this reason that it is reasonably simple for this Kiwi author to set out the future of England without any 'could-bes' or might-bes'.....

What Tony Learned From Down Under

This article from the British press in 1997, was presented by the President of the Adam Smith Institute. *"...We are only days into a Blair administration but a pattern is beginning to emerge."* Break quote.

Author's note - Of course it is. **Anybody who copies the proto-type will of necessity follow a pattern.**

Continue quote - *"Tony Blair and many of his key associates....have visited Australia and New Zealand have liked the good part of what they saw.*

We are beginning to see the first fruits of those visits. New Labour finds its inspiration not in the roots of the party's history in Britain, but from what has happened on the other side of the world.

...New Zealand did a blitzkrieg. Australia at a more measured pace.

...Our new Prime Minister has taken due note of their success.

...I do not want to spoil the party by reminding Mr Blair, that neither of those Labour governments managed to stay in office. He can console himself with the thought that their reforms have been accepted by their opponents and will not be reversed..." End quote.

Author's note - why is this? IMF conditions of course. There is no longer any choice in the matter.

Tony's Reforms

He has a massive job on his hands, and it has to be done in such a manner that the electorate is not quite sure what you are doing until you've done it.

A. Take farm subsidies away.
B. Divide British Post into 3 divisions 1. Banking 2. Postal 3. Telecom.
C. Completely destroy collective bargaining and unionism. Industrial reform.
D. Bring in the concept of workers all signing personal contracts.
E. Cut back viciously on welfare.
F. Tax reform. Bring in more money.
G. Stop funding education and health. Hospitals must go private. Schools make their own money and hire and fire teachers.
H. Sell out Great Britain little by little to overseas buyers.
I. Introduce secret agendas such as MAI.
J. Split up and sell up British Rail (BR).
K. Privatise and sell up the London underground.

His Promises

It was very interesting to be in Great Britain when Mr Blair made his initial speech. He had just been appointed Prime Minister and glowing with enthusiasm, he projected tremendous excitement.

'Daily Telegraph', 1ˢᵗ October 1997 - *"Mr Blair said the election of Labour had changed the nation's whole mood. He recalled driving from his home to Buckingham Palace..."The drive was so different...People watching our journey on T.V. came pouring out of the doorways, waving and shouting and clapping.*

They were liberated." Break quote.

Author's note - Oh dear - I smell terrible discouragement ahead.

Continue quote - *"He pledged "The money will be there. I promise you that. This year, every year. I will never countenance an NHS (National Health Service) that departs from its fundamental principle of health care based on need, not wealth."* Break quote.

Illustration

Author's note - I sit at my desk smiling quietly to myself. A story was told some years ago, of a brand-new politician in Africa, making his initial speech.

Polit - "I pledge to you that I will increase everybody's wages."
The crowd roared - "Oomdala."
Polit - "Housewives will receive the benefit."
Crowd - "Oomdala."
Polit - "Free education for all children."
Crowd - "Oomdala."
Polit - "Shorter working hours."
Crowd - "Oomdala."

Just as the political meeting was concluding a passing rubbish truck went over a bump in the road and spilt some of its load, a smelly green nauseating pile of rubbish.

An old African man passing by at that moment with his teenage son was heard to shout a warning, **"Be careful son. Don't step in the oomdala**."

Continue quote - *"He implored everyone to join his quest for a **new society**.*

*...But the Prime Minister insisted his Government was not asking everyone to change without changing itself. **He hoped that within five years, a quarter of dealings with Government could be done by a member of the public**, electronically through the television, telephone or computer...."* End quote.

Author's note - This is the first veiled hint that national governmental power is to be gradually phased out. This will make way for International Government or New World Order.

Unions Very Upset

From the same newspaper, we read - *"Speech Leaves Rank and File Cheesed Off.*

But for Tony's Blair's audience yesterday, it was hard cheese.

*Before him sat several thousand rank and file - the veteran doorsteppers, the **union warhorses**...*

*These people had come to hear an historic speech which would **reward the worker's struggle** during these long dark years of "Tory Misrule".*

What they heard however, was not aimed at them at all.

As the lights came up....most of the hall stood, but there were pockets of resistance, a heavy mob from the TGWU remained seated with arms crossed.

...Most of the messianic talk about modernisation was met in stony silence." Break quote.

Cold Reactions

Continue quote - *"...NEC member said, "It was glib of him to talk about hard choices. **They are not hard choices for the people who make them, they are hard for the people they impact on."*** End quote.

'Jerusalem Post', 2nd October 1996 - *"Blair vows to lead Britain into **new age**.*

"This is my covenant with the British people. Judge me on it. The buck stops with me. For the future, not the past. For the many, not the few. For trust, not betrayal. For the age of achievement, not the age of decline", the Labour leader said." Break quote.

Author's note - Please resist the urge to shout out 'Oomdala'. It makes you wonder who his speechwriter was. He had a great grasp of putting words together don't you agree?

Continue quote - *"Promising to lead "a great, radical, reforming government", Blair mapped out plans to create "a national grid of learning" by hooking up schools to the information super highway."* Break quote.

Author's note - There you go. More educational TWA - Time Wasting Activities. If they can't read or spell, what is the use of all this?

Continue quote - *"The speech was ecstatically received in the conference hall..."It was fantastic", said ....a 27 year old delegate. What he actually said is already well-known but it emphasised his vision. **He has a dream**."* End quote.

Author's note - **It's not his dream at all**!

A check on the Internet about the think tank, Adam Smith Institute, reveals that they awarded their servant, Tony Blair, 2 out of 3, for his first 200 days of fulfilling their plans.

What a good boy!

Enter One - Bill Clinton

"Blair, Clinton hail a new generation of politics." New Zealand 'Herald', 31ˢᵗ May 1997 - *"British prime Minister, Tony Blair, and United States President, Bill Clinton, cemented their warm personal relations yesterday by declaring themselves **political twins** from a new generation with no use for yesterday's ideology.*

*...Mr Clinton, visibly relaxed in Mr Blair's company, said there was an **"unbreakable alliance"** between the two countries."* Break quote.

Clinton Plans to Push Blair Towards Europe

Continue quote - *"Mr Clinton will leave Mr Blair in no doubt that "the future importance of the Anglo-American relationship will depend in large measure on the extent to which the UK accepts an integral role in the EU's development.*

...Mr Clinton is determined to take this matter of European integration to a new level, and this is where he will press Mr Blair and the other European leaders hardest " End quote. .

Author's note - Clinton is so under the thumb of his New World Organisers, he is to be seen here in a semi-diplomatic role of pushing England and Europe into **full political and monetary union**.

That is the gist of all this palaver!

Tony's Tasks

Just take a quick glance at all the work Mr Blair has ahead of him. He is first and foremost to destroy all that the British Labour Party has stood for. **If he follows the New Zealand role model, both he and his minister of finance will become two of the most unpopular men in history.**

Mankind never changes - remember?

"Friends today can be enemies tomorrow." P. Aristarchus.

Did you hear the phone ring?

Bill: "Hello Tony, it's Bill calling from the White House. At the moment, we are trying to drum up some interest in this Iraq affair. It's not easy, Tony. I mean, I'll be quite frank with you. I need a war - and pretty quickly. I have a few personal problems of my own and it's imperative that we focus peoples' attention on something else, preferably far away from home."

Tony: "I say, William, old man. I don't wish to be a stick in the proverbial mud but I have so many plans and such a lot to do at home. You know me - a likeable, jovial, friendly, positive person. You have been involved in this war business before - I haven't. I am not a war-monger (like your good self), and sincerely old man, I just seek time to destroy the British Unions with a little cunning dialogue and then I hope to turn Britain upside down. **"Reforms"**, I believe is the word."

Bill: "Listen, Tony. Our wives get on very well and that is half the battle won already. It won't last long, I'll see to that. Just a few planes, warships and a few thousand thrill-seeking able-bodied men and hey presto, mission accomplished!

Secondly, Tony, I wasn't going to mention this, but my bosses are pressing me to get on with it. Of course, you are aware that these guys are setting up a New World Order which means a global government. Their plans are almost completed, and the year 2000, is the target date. They follow the philosophies of that German thinker, **Hegel**, who made it clear that **"all historical events emerge from a conflict"**. This is a war we must have, Tony. Even if Saddam agrees to our terms, it is too late. There are too many folk who will be affected if we stop now e.g. our arms manufacturers. Why, I believe some of them have even opened new bank accounts to cope with the rapid increase in revenue.

By the way, Tony, I have many links to World Government groups and personalities

i.e. the Bilderbergers, the Trilateral Commission, the C.I.A., the Council on Foreign Relations, etc. What about your affiliations?"

Tony: "Oh yes, rather. There is a British secret society called **"The Group"**, or just plain **"Us"**. This society was founded at Oxford just as your "Order" was founded at Yale, but we lack the Masonic mumbo-jumbo. The Round Table, Rhodes scholars etc all have their part to play.

Oh, all right, Bill! I'll be a player, but give me some of the lime-light won't you? All 'press' is good 'press' provided it keeps us in the public eye."

Bill: Good man, Tony. I knew I could count on you. I've managed to scrape up a bit of semi-willing support from other countries who believe the lie, "If it comes from Uncle Sam, it's got to be good."

Why, even Australia and New Zealand, who are both absolutely broke at this moment of time, have agreed to come to the picnic. I hope Saddam doesn't get the news too quickly that New Zealand is joining in, or he may become terrified and give in before he even starts - "chortle, chortle!"

Tony: "Oh Bill, old man, you certainly have a wicked sense of humour!"

CHAPTER TWENTY

GOVERNMENTS OF THE WORLD IN THE HANDS OF GLOBAL PIRATES

In the year 1976, before he became President Clinton's Secretary of Defence, Lee Aspin signed the infamous, subversive document called **Declaration of Independence**.

Quote - *"Two centuries ago, our forefathers brought forth a new nation, now we must join with others to bring forth a new world order.*

All people are part of one global community...Our deepest obligation is to transmit to our posterity a planet richer in material bounty, in beauty and in delight than when we found it.

Narrow notions of national sovereignty must not be permitted to curtail that obligation...

We affirm that the economy of all nations is a seamless web...

We affirm that a world without law is a world without order, and we call upon all nations and its specialised agencies, and other institutions of world order, to broaden the jurisdiction of the World Court, that these may preside over a reign of law that will not only end wars, but end as well that mindless violence which terrorises our society, even in times of peace." End quote.

Bill Blythe, I mean Clinton, has been with three leading one world organisations.

- The CFR - The **Council on Foreign Relations**
- The TC - The **Tri-lateral Commission**
- The **Bilderbergers**

During the 1992 presidential campaign, Bill Clinton said that while he was at Georgetown University, he was greatly influenced by Professor Carroll Quigley, who wrote "Tragedy and Hope".

Quigley said he had "no aversion" to most of the plans of the network of **one-worlders** whose secret records he had been privy to. In a later book, he reveals that *"The (Rhodes) scholarships are merely a facade to conceal a secret society...."* End quote.

Attitudes to China

Be kind to China is the attitude of both Bush and Clinton. Why? What about the Tianeman Square massacre? Forget it. In world government terms, it is irrelevant. China makes up 1/4 of the world's population and therefore must be wooed into the New World Order plans.

Bill Clinton's visit to that country in June 1998, had as its aim, the softening up process, ready for China to be accepted in to the New World Order. This is highly important owing to China's massive population and its effect on world trade.

Rhodes Scholar, Richard Gardner, deputy assistant secretary of state for International Organisation Affairs, wrote in 'Foreign Affairs', April 1974 -
*"We are likely to do better by building our **"house of world order"** from the bottom up, rather than from the top down...an end run **around national sovereignty, eroding it piece by piece**, is likely to get us to world order faster than the old fashioned frontal attack."* End quote.

In 1890, Cecil Rhodes' said "universal peace" would begin, according to him, after one hundred years. In Autumn 1990, exactly one hundred years later, President Bush announced his New World Order.

The American Education Fellowship (begun by John Dewey) wrote in "Progressive Education", May 1949 edition, *"...teachers and school administrators (should) come to see themselves as **social engineers**. They must equip themselves as **change agents**."* End quote.

In 1948, Sir Julian Huxley wrote - "Its Purpose and its Philosophy".
*"...familiarise all peoples with the implications of the **transfer of full sovereignty from separate nations to a world organisation**."* End quote.

1951 - Disc jockey, Alan Freed, invents the phrase "rock and roll" which is a forerunner of rock music. Frank Zappa said, *"...the loud sounds and the bright lights of today are tremendous indoctrination tools."* End quote.

1952 - Aldous Huxley - "The Devils of London" is published. He writes *"...If exposed long enough to the tomtoms and the singing, every one of our philosophers would end by capering and howling like savages. Assemble a mob of men and women and treat them to amplified band music, bright lights....and in next to no time, **you can reduce them to a state of almost mindless subhumanity**. Never before have so few been in a position to make **fools**, **maniacs**, **or criminals** of so many."* End quote.

Author's note - Our children therefore, are the victims of social engineering, which explains why so many resemble **voodoo zombies** from a Carribean island. They can no longer look you in the eye and complete a whole sentence.

Perfect candidates for New World Order.

In 1957, occultist Alice Bailey, wrote "The Externalisation of the Hierarchy". She wrote - *"...the New World Order must be built (and) the three main channels through which the preparation for the new age is going on might be regarded as **the Church, the Masonic fraternity and the educational field**.*

*...The Masonic movement will meet the needs of those who can, and should, wield power. It is the custodian of the law, it is the home of the Mysteries, and the seat of Initiation. It holds in its symbolism the ritual of Deity, and **the way of salvation is pictorially preserved in all its work**. The methods of Deity are demonstrated in its Temples and **under the All-seeing eye its work can go forward**.*

It is a far more occult organisation than can be realised and is intended to be the training school for the coming advanced occultists..." End quote.

Author's note - **The Masonic way of salvation is unfortunately a way that leads to eternal separation from God. The Bible way of salvation is through Christ alone!**

*"For **by grace** are ye saved **through faith**; and that **not of yourselves**: it is the **gift of God: Not of works, lest any man should boast.** "*[1]

1973 - the 'Saturday Review of Education', 10th February, National Education Association (NEA) writes, *"...dramatic changes in the way we raise our children in the year 2000 are indicated...More than a dispenser of information, the teacher will be a conveyer of values, a philosopher. ...We will be agents of change."* End quote.

1976 - January/February issue of 'The Humanist', publishes an article by Professor Sheila Schwartz in which she expresses her thankfulness that, *"the crazies (fundamentalists) don't do all that much reading...If they did, they'd find out that they have already been defeated..."* End quote.

Author's note - It's a pity she doesn't do a little more reading herself. The Bible would tell her a whole different story. **It really depends on what you read!**

1991 - August - Librarian of Congress and former Rhodes Scholar, James Billington, writes from Moscow that, *"One of Russia's great art historians told me in all seriousness a year before (about August 1990) that all of Russia's troubles had begun when **Gorbachev was initiated into a Masonic Lodge**...during his first trip to London."* (Breakthrough to Hope - Moscow, August 1991.) End quote.

1991 - 15th July - Bob Heckman, one of the Bush re-election campaign's designated liaisons to the Religious Right sends a memo to his superior, Mimi Dawson, director of coalitions saying, *"The **President should avoid using the following phrase....New World Order...**"* End quote.

This is according to Michael Isikoff of the Washington 'Post' on the 11th October 1992, who says that, *"the **phrase began to disappear from Bush's vocabulary** shortly after (Pat) Robertson's book (The New World Order 1991) was published."* End quote.

Author's note - Too many people were learning the true meaning of this seemingly innocuous phrase.

It is a strange phenomenon but I have observed that those New World Order boys advertise almost every thing they are doing, at some time or another. It is just as though they cannot keep a secret and are **bursting to tell somebody**.

An experienced investigative reporter looks for the tiny cuttings in the newspaper. These are the ones which the average reader assumes (wrongly) are unimportant.

Poor old George - he blew his cover by repeating the phrase too many times.

1993 - In his book "The Twilight of Sovereignty", Walter Wriston declares, *"The world can no longer be understood as a collection of national economies, (but) a single global economy...**A truly global economy will require concessions of national power, and compromises of national sovereignty that seemed impossible a few years ago...**"* Break quote.

Wriston also speaks of a new international financial system....a new world money standard....a new world money market....the new world communications system," and he says, *"**There is no escaping the system**".* End quote.

1993 - 20th January - **Bill Clinton** takes the presidential oath and delivers his inaugural address saying *"....Let us resolve to make our government a place for what Franklin Roosevelt called, **"bold, persistent experimentation**....There is no longer a clear division between what is foreign and what is domestic, the world economy, the world environment, the world AIDS crisis, the world arms race. They affect us all.*

*Today **as an old order passes, the New World** is more free, but less stable...."* End quote.

Author's note - Clinton must have received prior warning not to mention the phrase New World Order. He just stopped himself in time.

As far as the New World Order is concerned, Saddam Hussein has been left to become a common international problem. At time of writing, in mid-1998, Bill Clinton is in serious trouble at home with his personal crises, so what could be better than a jolly good war against Saddam?

Some may ask "Why didn't they wipe him out the first time?" **They brushed away the cobwebs so that they could use the spider again.**

As we approach the year 2000, we remember the Hegelian Dialectic - *"All historical events emerge from a conflict between opposing forces."* End quote.

Thank you, Mr Hegel. Bill really appreciates your thoughts at this time.

Acknowledgement

Much of the information written up in pages 1-4 of this chapter was taken from the book - "Bill Clinton Will Continue The New World Order", by Dr Dennis L. Cuddy. We would **highly recommend** that you read this book. Please order from: The Southwest Radio Church Of The Air, P.O. Box 1144, Okalahoma City, Oklahoma 73101, U.S.A.

FOOTNOTE

[1]   Ephesians 2:8-9

CHAPTER TWENTY-ONE

1998

A strategic year, from many angles.

America signed its Declaration of Independence in 1776. Satanists who depend a great deal on occult numerology understand this simple sum.

1998
-1776

222 years or $2 + 2 + 2 = 6$ - the evil number.

Bill Clinton is the 42nd President of the U.S.A. - $4 + 2 = 6$.

Texe Marrs in his December 1997 Newsletter points out some very significant, previously hidden material.

"Global Rainbow Gatherings are to be held at sacred sites world-wide at 22 minutes past 2.00 a.m. (222) on the 22nd February (222) lasting for 2 hours and 22 minutes (222).

1998 is the 6th year after Bill Clinton's initial election.

1998 will be the 6th year since the FBI massacre at Waco, Texas.

1998, the UN celebrates its 51st birthday $5 + 1 = 6$." End quote.

In an earlier chapter, we learned that America was settled by Freemasons and occultists for a **peculiar and particular purpose** known only to the initiated few.

Whether you, the reader, believes in witchcraft or not, is completely irrelevant at this time in history. A satanic plan is already being worked out and we can be sure that the U.S.A. is at the forefront of this plan.

Rumours Abound

N.B. 'The Intelligence Digest', 30th January 1998, reports that *"The American army has been cut by 44% since 1991, from 18 divisions to 10. Of the remaining divisions, one is committed to Bosnian peacekeeping, with another in reserve, whilst three are in Korea. An internal Senate memorandum on the state of the American military has warned that the army is suffering "extremely serious" readiness problems...."* End quote.

MAI (Multilateral Agreement on Investment)

The OECD hope that this will be introduced to New Zealand, possibly during 1998. Overseas companies will then move their investments to this country and buy up every lucrative business and service. If the New

Zealand government holds them up in any manner, after the agreement has been signed, they can be taken to the World Court and sued.

Good old New Zealand - another first. Guinea-pigs again!

Change of Anthem Necessary

I sincerely believe we must change the words of our National anthem to:

"God defend New Zealand from unscrupulous multi-nationals."

Government No Longer Requires Foreign Investment Group

New Zealand 'Herald', 22nd January 1998 - *"The Foreign Direct Investment Advisory Group, which was formed to advise and inform the Government **and the public** on international investment issues **has been disbanded**."* Break quote.

Author's note - The reason for this is clear. The powers that be do not want the public to know anything about this seditious bill.

Continue quote - *"The disbanding was because the group's services were no longer seen as necessary....*

***The public now accepted the need for foreign investors** and one of the more vocal critics of the investment when the group was formed, W.....n P....s, was now more sympathetic to it."* Break quote.

Author's note - He initially was vehemently against it. He now understands that he is powerless to stop overseas investors and has been clearly informed, **"Go along with the plans or down the road you go."**

Continue quote - *"...The task of promoting foreign direct investment now rests with the Ministry of Foreign Affairs and Tradenz. The latter is more involved in promoting sectors to specific investors, while the former's job is to tell foreigners what a great investment destination New Zealand is.*

*...During its tenure, (the advisory group), its main message was that **international investments did not threaten the country's sovereignty** but helped provide jobs, technology transfer and gave broader access for New Zealand products and services."* End quote.

Author's note - **Why did these government spokesmen feel that they needed to bring up the question of New Zealand's sovereignty?** They know that some of us know the truth.

New Zealand and 1998

The plan is to sell it up as quickly as possible.

Australia and 1998

John Howard will introduce legislation to defeat the unions. Later, the plan is to sell the country out as quickly as possible, including Telstra.

1998 - Israel's 50th Jubilee

The observance of this jubilee was officially launched on the 23rd December, 1997, the first night of Hanukkah. Because of the International date line, John Howard, Australia's Prime Minister, was the first to light a candle. Others who also lit candles were British Prime Minister, Tony Blair, Canadian Prime Minister, Jean Cretien, Italian President, Oskar Luigi Scalfaro, Czech President, Vaclav Havel and U.S. President, Bill Clinton.

Don't forget that the 14th May 1948, was the day that independence came in Israel. The Jewish prophet, Isaiah, wrote in about the year 740 B.C. - *"Who hath heard such a thing? Who hath seen such things? Shall the earth be made to bring forth in one day? Or shall a nation be born at once? For as soon as Zion travailed, she brought forth her children."*[1] End quote.

On the wall of my office, I have hung the front page of the 'Palestine Post', dated 16th May 1948, and the headline is **"State of Israel is Born"**.

Jubilee Events

In ancient Israel, on the tenth day of the seventh month, the trumpet sounded. Liberty was proclaimed. All slaves returned to their families. There was to be no sowing or reaping. Land was to be returned to its original owners.

Keep your eye on Israel in 1998. Their Jubilee is to be celebrated for the first time in 2000 years. **What will happen this year**?

Not only that, at this particular time in history as a 2000 year period called "The Times of the Gentiles" comes to a conclusion, **God has promised to remove the spiritual veil from Jewish eyes.**

Many of them, starting as from this year, will begin to recognise Jesus Christ the Lord as God's Son and as their long awaited Messiah.

"For I would not brethren that ye should be ignorant of this mystery, lest ye should be wise in your own conceits that blindness in part is happened to Israel, until the fulness of the Gentiles be come in."[2] End quote.

Author's note - **A simple English translation of the above passage.** Don't try and be clever, using your own weak human intellect to work all this out. The reason that the Jews as a nation get so uptight about the Lord Jesus Christ, is that God Himself has put a temporary blindness on many of them. This blindness is so that non-Jews (called Gentiles) have about 2000 years to accept God's offer of salvation through the precious blood of His Lamb, the Lord Jesus Christ. **Therefore, our advice to any non-Jew reading this book is "You'd better hurry up. Your time is quickly running out. The 2000 year period is almost finished**!"

Very shortly, many in Israel will give up their proud, secular, style of living and become very spiritually aware.

'Jerusalem Post', 10th November 1997 - *"Kissinger: It's time for final settlement with the Palestinians.*

*Former U.S. Secretary of State, Henry Kissinger, said yesterday, it is now time to tackle a "**number of big issues**" in the Middle East peace process - including the fact that a Palestinian state is inevitable.*

*Since universal recognition of that state is inevitable, "**the question becomes what are its borders?**", Kissinger said in a lecture to a packed auditorium in Tel Aviv's Habimah Theatre. He said that although he had been the first to advocate the step-by-step process to the Arabs and Israelis, now he believes it is **time for bigger steps, or for a negotiated final settlement**.*

"But the first, the essential requirement for peace, is knowing where you want to go", Kissinger said. "If you do not know the destination, you cannot get there, and each step, each concession, becomes harder."

*...His subject was, "**United States and Middle Eastern Policy in a changing Global Arena**".*

*...Nobel Peace laureate, Kissinger, who was Secretary of State under Presidents Nixon and Ford, became known as the **father of shuttle diplomacy** when he negotiated the cease-fire agreements between Israel, Egypt and Syria following the Yom Kippur War.*

*... "I told Begin on the day after Camp David and have said it ever since, that the key question is, what borders will that unit have. These two issues must be faced - **the borders**, and in return, **the recognition of a Palestinian state cannot be prevented**, whatever Israel thinks."*

*Kissinger said, "**It is clear** Israel cannot return to the 1967 borders, so without tying myself to any particular line, I think something like the Allon Plan will be the outcome."* End quote.

FOOTNOTES

[1]   Isaiah 66:8
[2]   Romans 11:25

150

CHAPTER TWENTY TWO

RUSSIA AND THE NEW WORLD ORDER

When the ex-minister of finance in New Zealand completed his task of following the IMF loans, conditions, and selling out of New Zealand's sovereignty, he then began to travel world-wide. His task was to explain to other nations, **how to do it**. One of his first ports of call was **Russia.**

Wreck your own country first of all, then look around for other countries to wreck.

New Zealand 'Herald', 20th February 1992 - *"The former Minister of Finance.....is off soon to talk to the Russians about **privatisation**. He expects to leave on March 1 for discussions.....said **he would be a part of a 3 man privatisation advisory committee organised by the World Bank**. He was appointed a consultant to the bank in March 1990."* End quote.

Author's note - What does all this tell us?

i. The privatisation scheme was not dreamed up by this man.

ii. He lost his job, ultimately, through the rushing through of these wrecking policies.

iii. If you serve your New World Order masters well, you can always be upgraded by them at a later date. After all, who wants to struggle with one small nation's economy when you can fly world-wide, first class at that, under the auspicious name of the World Bank. Oh, the power and the glory!

The Result of His Policies

'European', 31st August - 6th September 1995 - *"Russian bank crisis may spark a return to dictators.*

Economists in Russia say that the country's banking crisis is so critical that it could lead to political upheaval and an eventual return to dictatorship.

...The run on the banks by depositors demanding their money back would effectively paralyse the monetary system. Businesses would then be unable to pay wages, taxes or debts, the state, without taxes, would be unable to meet its obligations, and .....some sort of Pinochet would step in to restore order, an allusion to the former Chilean dictator." End quote.

What Was the Ultimate Result?

'Australian', 23rd September 1996 - *"IMF sets provisos on billions for Russia.*

The International Monetary Fund agreed in principle on Thursday to grant Russia a multi-billion dollar loan, provided certain conditions were met...." Break quote.

Author's note - Here we go again. How many more illustrations do we need to prove that it is the same old scenario over and over again.

Continue quote - *"Mr....quoted by Itar Tass news agency, was speaking during a break in negotiations with the IMF director general, Mr Michel Comdessus, on the loan, expected to total at least $US9 billion....spread over three years.*

The Russian central bank said it hopes to get $US12 billion from the IMF, which would make it the second largest credit in the IMF's history after that granted to Mexico.

...The key loan is aimed at consolidating market reforms.

...Mr....said, the Government was ready to remove taxes on exports of oil and gas this year - one of the conditions the IMF insisted on for the loan.

...The IMF wants Russian domestic oil and gas prices to match the higher prices on the world market." End quote.

Author's note - This is outrageous! Just because the Russians were enjoying lower prices, these IMF rascals insist on a price rise which makes it harder on the domestic Russian consumer.

It's simply not fair!

Who was it that said, *"The triumphing of the wicked is short."*[1]

The Russian Invasion of Israel

Up on a mountain above the town of Tiberias, a small group of Messianic Jews and friends gather Sabbath by Sabbath. Overlooking the spectacular Sea of Galilee, I had the privilege of addressing this group.

When the meeting had concluded, a young Jewish boy asked me a question. "Mr Smith, do you think the Russians will invade Israel, before or after the **peace treaty**?"

This question was simple to answer as I have been asked it so many times before.

The prophecy which outlines in great detail the future of Israel was written down soon after 593 B.C.

After the Peace Treaty

The invasion of Israel will take place just after the peace treaty has been signed, and the Israeli's are living in peace. The Russian armies, along with their allies, will invade Israel.

"Thus saith the Lord God, it shall also come to pass that at the same time shall things come into thy mind, and thou shalt think an evil thought.

*And thou shalt say, I will go up to the land of **unwalled villages**. I will go to them that **are at rest**, that dwell safely, all of them **dwelling without walls**, and **having neither bars nor gates** to take a spoil."*[2] End quote.

Which Nations Will Invade Israel?

Russia, Iran, Ethiopia, Libya, Germany, Turkey and many of the Moslem armies.

An Outline of the Invasion

1. The initial thrust comes from the north i.e. Russia.
2. Of all the troops who come, none will return home again.
3. A supernatural calamity will hit all these invaders.
4. They will fall all over the land of Israel.
5. The people of Israel will use their enemies weapons and equipment as firewood. This supply will last them for seven years.
6. The bodies of the now dead invaders will cause a terrible stench of death throughout the land. Not only that, this will cause a health hazard. People passing through the country will need to block their noses.
7. Every Israeli citizen will be required to become involved in the general clean-up. This full time exercise will take seven months in the initial stages.
8. When the seven months is up, certain individuals will be employed by the Israeli government to continue to search for, and bury bodies and bones as they find them. These searchers, when leaving their home towns, along with all travellers throughout the land of Israel, will be required to carry shovels and little sign posts in their vehicles. If one finds even a bone, and has no time to bury it, he will put up a little sign, **"Bone here",** and the burial squad will come along with their shovels and complete the job.
9. Birds of prey will have a mighty feast.
10. The name of the God of Israel will be magnified as every world citizen recognises, maybe for the first time, that Almighty God is indeed alive and well.

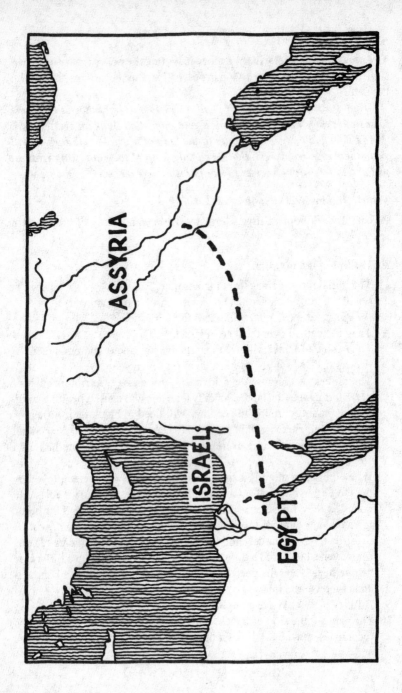

What Spirit is Controlling Russia?

In his magazine, 'Prophetic Vision', David Hathaway, a committed Christian believer in the Lord Jesus Christ, tells of his supernatural experience.

"My first visit to Siberia in 1993 was to Chita, and in a meeting in the local Culture House, I came face to face with the demon controlling Russia. A group of intercessors were behind the stage curtains with me, but after they left to begin the service, I stayed.

*Feeling led, I drew back a curtain and there, in the darkness, was a bust of Lenin about the same height as I am. Then I saw a green light glow in his eyes, and I had the most unusual experience of evil. **I heard the image speak, saying, "I am the son of Lucifer. Everyone thinks I am dead, but I am not. I am alive and I control Russia."***

Any person who believes the lie "Communism is dead" is easily fooled. True, twice born believers in Jesus Christ are still followed around by the secret police." End quote.

Many years ago, I heard an elderly missionary, a Mr Dashfield, recounting his adventures whilst visiting Moscow.

He joined the line of people waiting to view Lenin's body which was, and still is, kept in a preserved state. As he looked at the corpse through its glass lid, a guard standing nearby said, "That is comrade Lenin. He is kept is very good condition, isn't he?"

Mr Dashfield replied, "Yes, but I notice that he is dead. **The One that I serve, the Lord Jesus Christ, was dead but is now alive again.**

The guard laughed and said, "You Christians are crazy, as are your beliefs. You talk about a resurrection from the dead, but we Communists know that that is absolutely impossible. Minerals are running out world-wide, and therefore, there would not be enough to go around. For example, there is no way there would be enough phosphorus.

Mr Dashfield smiled as he replied - **"The Bible says that at the resurrection, the dead in Christ will rise first. Then you Communists will have to scratch around for your own phosphorus!"**

FOOTNOTES

[1]   Job 20:5

[2]   Ezekiel 38:11

CHAPTER TWENTY-THREE

THE MILLENNIUM BUG

(Date of writing - 22ⁿᵈ May 1988)

The clock strikes midnight. The date is 31ˢᵗ December 1999.

Suddenly, the lights go out in each country, one after the other. Citizens fortunate enough to possess lamps and candles light them, if they also had forethought to have a box of matches in the house.

Someone mutters "Another jolly power cut. They shouldn't have privatised the government electricity department. Anybody for a cup of coffee? It's quite romantic really - coffee by candle-light. Hello, what's going on? There's no water coming from the taps."

Another voice shouts from the bathroom. "Dad, why doesn't the toilet flush? What's happening?"

This book was not written with the purpose of terrifying people but to enlighten readers as to the true state of affairs in the world today. What you have just read is peanuts compared to other scenarios that will become more obvious as the new year progresses.

Lies - Lies - Lies

Because men generally prefer darkness to light, readers of this, our 6ᵗʰ book, will rapidly discover, to their horror, that what they thought was taking place in the world, is not necessarily taking place at all.

The Most Obvious Lie...

...being propagated at the time of writing is that the new millennium commences at 12:01 a.m. 1ˢᵗ January 2000. This is simply not true, in spite of the fact that celebrations are being held by government agencies and others, worldwide.

The year 2000 is the end of this thousand year period, or millennium.

Those in authority at the Royal Observatory at Greenwich, which is situated on the banks of the River Thames, tell us that **the new millennium starts at 12:01 a.m., 1ˢᵗ January 2001**. Now, there's a shock for some of you!

'Newsweek', 2ⁿᵈ June 1997 - "*The Day the World Shuts Down.*

Y2K (official name for the Millennium Bug) could be the event that could all but paralyse the planet." End quote.

The Problem

Over 30 years ago, when computers appeared on the world scene, programmes were recorded on Hollerith Cards. This card was made of stiff cardboard with only 80 spaces for memory. This being the case, **to save space, the programmers entered the dates using only 2 digits instead of 4 i.e. 1947 = 47, 1999 = 99. Therefore, at midnight on the 31st December 1999, the dates will flick over to 00. This simply means that the mainframe computers world-wide, which, owing to the fact that they cannot reason, will assume the date is now 1900 and shut down.**

The Asian races, some of them working under their own time systems, are assuming wrongly that the problem is peculiarly western, and as they are working under "emperor time", they will be okay.

Bad News

The computer knows nothing about differing ideas on time and works according to the system programmed into it. In most cases, this would be G.M.T., or Greenwich Mean Time. This being the case, the country of New Zealand would have approximately 12 extra hours up its sleeve, and the crash should take place there at about 12:00 noon, 1st January 2000.

The country of Samoa however, the last country in the world to receive the sun each day, would have its computers go down earlier; possibly at approximately 12:00 noon or thereabouts, on 31st December 1999.

Total World Wide Chaos

The world has never been this way before and the majority of people in most countries will be totally unprepared.

Solving the Problem

This is completely out of the question. Even if a giant car manufacturer, for example, managed to make their mainframe computer compliant, if a small factory down the road which manufactured ball-bearings for the wheels had its computer go down, there obviously would be no more motor-cars from that factory. So many computers are linked that if one made a mistake, the others would build on that mistake and collapse.

Change the Dates

Unfortunately this is not possible as many of the dates cannot be found.

They are encoded into lines on the computer and in many cases, **the codes have been lost or the programmers have died**.

Put New Dates on the Computer

This is not possible either as **there is no international agreement on dating format**. Which system would be used - English or American?

Should Governments Work to Update their Computers?

No, not at all. If one down the road is not compliant, it will crash the one that you have just spent millions of dollars upgrading.

Why is the Media Not Warning Us?

To avoid **panic** setting in as this problem is so big. People could not handle it. It will only become more apparent as we approach the dates mentioned.

Could the Collapse Commence Earlier?

Yes! Some soft-ware manufacturers have arranged for their equipment to become obsolete earlier than 31 December 1999 e.g. a popular date for some is 9th September 1999. This equals 9.9.99. The purpose for this of course is **planned obsolescence**. This makes way for updated software, and therefore, more sales. Also it needs to be borne in mine that some software manufacturers have used these numbers to terminate certain computer data.

Which Areas of Society Will be Affected?

Not so much the desk-top PC's but the older mainframes that many groups are trying so desperately to upgrade. The PC's use silicon chips which can be easily replaced but not so the older mainframes. **Forty-five thousand worldwide are due for collapse**.

Social Security	Tax payments	Bills
Pensions	Tax refunds	Loans
Medicare	Seniority	Military
Retirement Benefits	Over-time	Navigation
Driving Licences	Credit cards	National power grid
Voter registration	Interest due dates	City water
School grades	Delinquent accounts	City sewerage
Salary increases	Bonuses	Trains and tracks

Tax codes   Commissions   Train movements
Mortgages   Signals and switches   Insurance
Air Traffic control   Aircraft   Traffic lights
Motor cars

No goods   No deliveries
No lights in stores   No bills
No business

How long will this drug be safe?
Machine maintenance
When was this product built?
How long is this invoice overdue?
Has this subscription expired?
Enrolment in schools and universities
Car rental agencies - they accept drivers' licences that expire in the future.

The 'McAlvany Intelligence Advisor', March 1998 lists more detail for us to consider.

1. There is not a single airline in the world which is compliant.
2. KLM Royal Dutch Airlines will ground all aircraft on 1.1.2000.
3. Al Italia will ground all aircraft on 1.1.2000.
4. Other airlines will quickly follow suit.
5. Insurance companies are saying this is not an 'act of God', and therefore will not pay out.
6. Arthur Grass, who was the IRS computer trouble-shooter for the USA has resigned for a better opportunity in private industry. *"His replacement or successor will face the biggest technology management challenge in the world."* End quote.
7. Already in the U.S. a quiet run has begun on food reserves.
8. Lights will go out, food will run out, fuel will dry up.
9. If the U.S. computers can no longer talk to each other, the trains will stop as will the U.S. economy.
10. Today there is no manual railroad switching system.
11. None of the U.S. railroads will be compliant by 31st December 1999.
12. Coal will not be transported even during winter.
13. Heating oil will become unavailable.
14. Food will rot in railway wagons.
15. Union Pacific, the biggest in the U.S. carries 350,000 carloads of freight on a normal day.
16. UPS - United Parcel Service will be unable to operate.

17. 169,000 airline take-offs and landings in the U.S. each day. They will all stop.
18. Boeing 747s or 767s can have **up to 500 computers in operation on board**.
19. **This author will not be flying anywhere during this period.**
20. IBM, which built air traffic control systems says they should not be used beyond December 1999.
21. Radar and tracking systems will go down.
22. Therefore passenger and cargo flights will cease.
23. The U.S. military depends on computers for planes, missiles, bombs, submarines, tanks, satellites, ships, air defence systems not made public interact or are controlled by date sensitive computer chips.
24. In early 1997, the Department of Defence admitted it had **13,897 computer systems** and none of them was Millennium Bug compliant.

Author's note - **This looks like a very suitable time for Russia or Iraq, or even Iran to launch a chemical or biological attack against America**. (See our book 'Better Than Nostradamus'.)

25. GPS - Global Positioning Satellites will be affected.
26. Communications will be in chaos.
27. Fishing boats using GPS will suffer also.
28. **The taxation system will go down**. They have been trying to fix it for 30 years.
29. The IRS meltdown could begin as early as 1st July 1999.
30. When the public begins to learn this fact, the more unscrupulous may cease paying taxes to the government.

This is called '**non-compliance**'. Many government people are becoming very nervous as a result.

31. Social Security cheques will not be sent out.
32. With bad data, Medicare could go bankrupt.
33. Most American cities have only **4-5 days of food on grocery shelves**. Restocking will depend on truck movement. The trucks however, will not deliver food, as social unrest will make it too dangerous for the truck-drivers.
34. Restaurants also depend on food deliveries and will suffer a similar fate.
35. Lights at bridges and tunnels will go out.
36. Police computers will go down and shootings, hijackings and robberies will go up.

37. Grain shipments to farms and poultry establishments will be hit hard. Animals and poultry will suffer as a result.

38. **ATM's will go down.**

Proof - Proof - Proof

Check your credit card dates for expiry. If they have only 2 digits e.g. 00 or even 02, it makes no difference. Your money supply will stop at the end of 1999, if not sooner as the computer thinks 1900 instead of the year 2000.

Sad but true. Sorry folks.

By now, some readers are saying, **"Stop the world, I want to get off!"**

No, you don't. Keep reading. Every problem has a simple answer which you will later find within the pages of this book.

39. Riots will be a natural result.

40. Martial law will be declared and FEMA invoked.

FEMA = Federal Emergency Management Act. This puts all power into the hands of the President of the USA.

41. **New York** in particular has been singled out as a city with massive problems to be revealed at this time. (See our book 'Better Than Nostradamus'.)

42. Lawyers will be overrun with litigation cases.

43. People will immediately wish to blame someone else.

David Rockefeller, one of the major globalist leaders said "*We are on the verge of a global transformation. All we need is the right major crisis and the nations will accept the New World Order.*" End quote.

Prophetically speaking, **we await the revealing of a one-world powerful dictator**. He is alive, even as we write, and is waiting for the best time to reveal himself.

"*And now you know what withholdeth that he might be revealed in his own appointed time.*" [1]

Advice - Watch the media and collect your own data on this very imminent and earth-shattering phenomenon. **Above all, don't be afraid. Help is at hand!**

Here is a letter from the 'Jerusalem Post' that was sent to some friends of ours:

"*Dear Mr and Mrs Anderson*

Because of your letter of March 18th, your subscription expires March 27th 2000, but because of technical difficulties, our computers don't accept dates beyond 31st December 1999.

However, we do keep strict written records, so when we have solved the problem with the year 2000, we will be able to up-date our computers correctly.

We apologise for the inconvenience this might have caused you.

Yours sincerely

....
International Edition"

A Note In Passing for the Sceptics

Please consider this excerpt taken from "The Globalisation of World Politics - An Introduction to International Relations", edited by John Baylis and Steve Smith, and published by Oxford University Press in 1997.

*"Our......governments......seem to be in perpetual states of **crisis**! However, in the context of the world-system, Wallerstein wishes to reserve the term to refer to a very specific temporal occurrence. For him, a crisis **constitutes a unique set of circumstances that can only be manifested once in the lifetime of a world system**. It occurs when the contradictions, the secular trends and the cyclical rhythms at work within that system combine in such a way as to mean that **the system cannot continue to reproduce itself**. Thus, **a crisis within a particular world-system heralds its end and replacement by another system**."* End quote.

The world system that we have functioned under for many years now has up until now, on the whole, continued in a very smooth pattern. Countries were self-sufficient to varying degrees i.e. Britain - basically totally self-sufficient owing to the very strong traditional system that governed it, while the various African nations were not quite as strong owing to relief needs etc. However, all these nations were still run by their own governments and held their own sovereignty.

The New World Order advocates know that to bring in another world system would not be possible unless some dreadful crisis or catastrophe occurred worldwide as mentioned in the above article. There is no way that the orderly and methodical British would suddenly hand over the reins of their country to just anybody, nor would the Americans whose national pride is very strong and who, when challenged, would defend themselves to the hilt.

It is this author's belief that the millennium bug could be the catalyst that will herald the end of the present world system and see in the

next one. Because the **undermining groundwork** has already been done by the traitors in the Parliaments of most countries, and because there is absolutely **nothing that can be done** by anybody to fix this bug, there will be no recourse for these countries but to **give in to whoever holds the key to the problem**.

The Christchurch 'Press', on the 6th June 1998, gives us further information on this event that is about to take place at the end of 1999.

"The oldest timekeeping machine in the world to suffer from the millennium bug has been found in a museum in Liverpool.

The 400 year old instrument, which predicts the position of the planets, will stop working at the dawn of the new millennium, unable to accept the date of January 1 2000.

The equatorial, built by an unknown craftsman in 1600, predicts the position of the sun, moon, other planets, and even eclipses, through a system of rotating disks and arms. But the last date inscribed was 1999.

"It must have seemed like an eternity at the time", said the museum's curator...." End quote.

A Final Statement

The clock ticks and the hands move on into January 1, 2000.

At that point the economy, as we know it today, will cease to exist.

The stage will then be set for the introduction of the **mark of the beast** i.e. a silicon chip implanted in the right hand or the forehead.

"And he causeth all, both small and great, rich and poor, free and bond, to receive a mark in their right hand, or in their foreheads:

And that no man might buy or sell, save he that had the mark, or the name of the beast, or the number of his name.

Here is wisdom. Let him that hath understanding count the number of the beast: for it is the number of a man; and his number is Six hundred, threescore and six."[2] Predicted in 96 A.D.

We're here - we've arrived!

Get yourself right with God!

What Do We Do?

A precedent has been set for us in the book of Genesis Chapters 41 and 42.

God's man Joseph, being in an influential position in the land of Egypt was able to collect and store grain for the seven years of drought the Lord had warned him lay ahead.

166

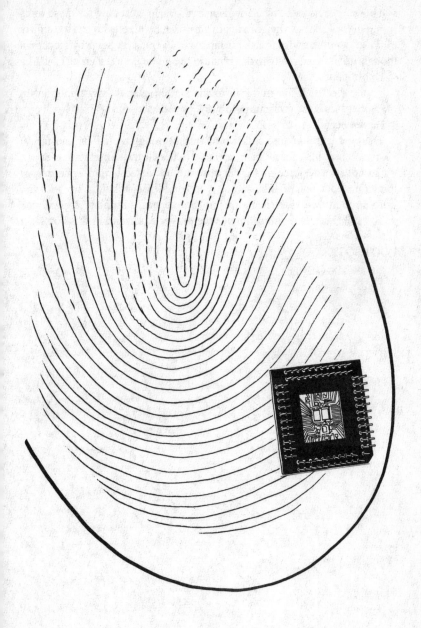

This story acts as a "type" or Jewish Midrashic teaching for those of us living in these days. Any born again Christian believer who has the ability to do so would be wise to use his land wisely and store up provisions in a thoughtful manner, ready to distribute at the given time. 1 Tim. 6:17-19.

Don't Panic!

To the vast majority living in towns and cities it is very important to memorise two sets of scriptures - Phil.4:19 and Matt. 6:31-33.

Remember

The God who took the children of Israel through the wilderness for 40 years and provided for all their needs - **He is still the same!**

Do not fear. Rejoice in a great opportunity to see Him do marvellous things on your behalf. The secret is to establish a relationship with the Lord through the experience of being "born again" - nothing else will do!

To establish this relationship see the prayer at the end of this book.

FOOTNOTES

[1] II Thessalonians 2:6

[2] Revelation 13:16-17

ANNOUNCING THE BIRTH OF THE NEW WORLD ORDER (WITHOUT GOD), UNDER THE ALL-SEEING EYE OF SATAN, THE ANTI-CHRIST, 666

CHAPTER TWENTY-FOUR

THE GREAT PYRAMID OF GIZA - AN AMAZING DISCOVERY

The air was dank and stale, as we left the light of the outside world, passed some Egyptian doorkeepers dressed in caftans, and inched our way along the stone floor of the passageway. The sense of age, the permanence of time, the smell, the sweaty hand-marks on the walls, all spoke eloquently of man, always seeking for meaning to life's many mysteries. They had come here, thousands of them, year after year, to experience for themselves a personal revelation in viewing one of the seven wonders of the world.

This author was one such person. After three visits to the site, I became convinced that there was more to this structure than met the eye. Some said it was New Age, or occult, or weird, because Michael Jackson slept under one. Others thought it was a burial tomb for the Pharaohs but I was not convinced.

3 Important Questions

Q. Why is there a picture of the Great Pyramid of Giza on the reverse side of every US$1 bill, post 1933?

Q. Why did George Bush, a member of the Skull and Bones Club at Yale University, say "Barbara and I will meet you at the Great Pyramid at the turn of the century"?

Q. Has the Great Pyramid at Giza something to do with the ancient prophecies?

Astounding Findings

1. **Position** - Its architect obviously had a knowledge of the position of the poles as the building is oriented true north. After 4,000 years, it is only off 3 minutes and that is mainly due to subsidence. (N.B. A minute is a bare fraction of a degree.)

2. The Great Pyramid was placed in the exact centre of all the land area of the world.

3. It was never meant to be a burial place for the Pharaohs or anybody else. The 2nd and 3rd pyramids served this purpose.

4. **It was not built by the Egyptians** but according to Herodotus, **by "strangers to Egypt"**. Could it be that Peleg was involved? "...in his

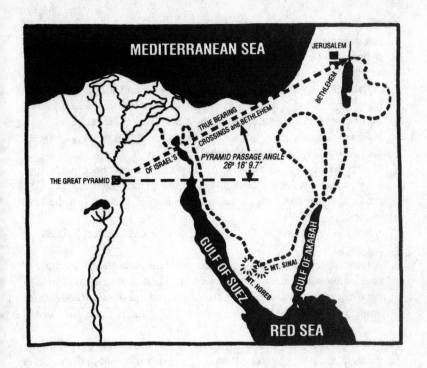

THE GREAT PYRAMID AT GIZA
DIVIDES THE EARTH'S LAND AREA
INTO 4 EQUAL PARTS ie NW=NE=SW=SE

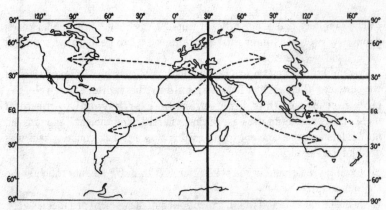

days was the earth divided." Something divided the earth that would not destroy its unity.

5. It has now been discovered that the Great Pyramid divides the land surfaces of the world into equal parts i.e. All the land to the east is equal to the land to the west and to the north and south. North-east equals north-west, south-east equals south-west, south-east equals north-east, south-west equals north-west... - see illustration.

6. It was used as a sundial for the whole land of Egypt as its position on the earth's surface made it extremely accurate.

7. It was originally covered with a white limestone plaster-like substance that reflected the sunlight right over the land of Egypt. That protective coat has now, in the main, fallen off, leaving just the bare stones.

8. Some have said that the Great Pyramid is the most perfect building in the world.

9. A reasonable **knowledge of geometry and mathematics** is essential in the finding out of its mysterious secrets. These mysteries are found in symbol, measure and angle, e.g. from its base a line drawn at one precise angle intersects the Red Sea crossing, Bethlehem and the Jordan River crossing.

10. The angle of the slope on the pyramid's sides is known as the pyramidic pi angle and is 51 degrees 51' 14.3". No other pyramid in the world is built at this angle.

Why?

The architect had a magnificent mind. Any reader who understands geometry, please explain this marvellous fact to readers who do not understand geometry.

It is doubtful if any human being could have possibly designed this. **If we consider the height of the pyramid as the radius of a circle, the circumference of that circle would be exactly equal to the total measurement around the base of the pyramid**. The ancient Egyptians did not understand the concept of pi, as this was a Greek concept, and was used later in history.

11. Exciting information you will agree, yet this still has not touched the main issue.

12. Is the Great Pyramid of Giza mentioned in the ancient prophecies?

Yes, it most certainly is!

Prophecy given about 740 B.C. now becomes relevant in the years 1998-2000.

*"In that day, shall **there be an altar to the Lord** in the midst of the land of Egypt and **a pillar at the border thereof**, to the Lord.*

*And it shall be **a sign and for a witness unto the Lord of Hosts** in the land of Egypt...."* [1] End quote.

13. The word 'Giza' in Arabic is the word for **edge** or **border**. A literal translation means - "The Great Pyramid of the border." It is right on the border of southern and northern Egypt and divides the world's land mass in to 4 equal parts.

14. This great pyramid is:
    a. An **altar** to the Lord.
    b. It is a **pillar** to the Lord.
    c. It is situated on the border.
    d. It is a **sign and a witness**, to the Lord of Hosts, in the land of Egypt.

15. The Freemasons and occultists revere it for a peculiar reason, yet it does not belong to them.

16. In order to interpret its symbolism, there is a key which must be followed.

In a prophecy given between the years 593-571 B.C., God's Word to the prophet was,

"I have appointed thee each day for a year."

Notice please that the code changes slightly for measuring the pyramid.

17. N.B. **The Great Pyramid key. 1 inch = 1 year of history.**
a) the actual height of the Great Pyramid is 5449 inches.
b) the distance from the Pyramid's entrance right to the extremity of the interior passages and chambers is also equal to 5449 inches.
c) In the original Hebrew language in which the O.T. was written, each Hebrew letter has a numeric value. When added together, the value of all the letters used in the prophecy is 5449. (Isaiah 19:19-20).

A threefold cord is not quickly broken.

A History Book in Stone

18. **A road map of history** - a 6000 year calendar. This monument to the Lord in the land of Egypt is an historical monument. As one goes in the doorway with a measuring tape, using **the key as 1 pyramid inch for a year** there are immediately 3 important events dated for us.

God's **law** to Moses given on Mount Sinai, then there is the date for the **birth of Christ**, then the date for the **crucifixion**.

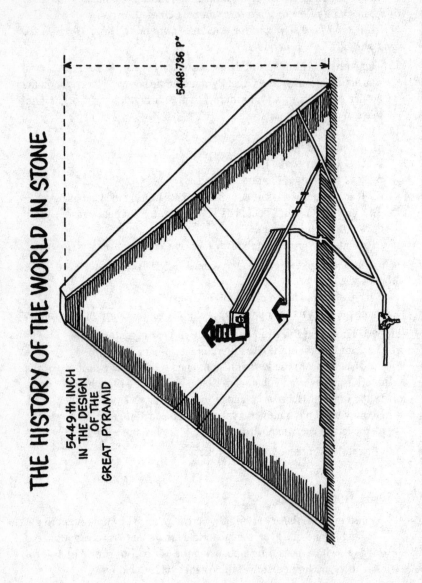

THE HISTORY OF THE WORLD IN STONE

5449th INCH
IN THE DESIGN
OF THE
GREAT PYRAMID

5448·736 P"

19. Notice the 3 main parts to understand the 3 events listed above. Look at the chart provided and observe -

a.   The first ascending passage.
b.   The grand gallery.
c.   The King's chamber.

These passages therefore provide a time line, taking history through the three stages already mentioned, and on through the dates for -

1.   World War I
2.   World War II
3.   **The King's Chamber, a representation of Heaven**. This is the ultimate goal of every intelligent man and woman.
4.   The dates appear to run out about the year 2,000.

19. Unfortunately, there is also a descending passage which runs downhill in the opposite direction (see chart). It has exactly the same length or representative time span and finishes at the **Subterranean Chamber, known as The Pit - a representation of Hell.**

20. N.B. This is not to say history stops in the year 2,000 yet obviously, a certain period of history closes at this point. **Could it be the times of the Gentiles?**

But wait, we haven't touched on the main point yet!

21. **THE GREAT PYRAMID OF GIZA ON THE BORDER HAS NO CAPSTONE.**

People have searched for it but it is simply missing.

22. Why? The true capstone of history will be revealed at the appropriate time.

23. In the meantime the US$1 bill designed by a secret society called **the "Illuminati", have provided their own capstone**. (See our fifth book, "Better Than Nostradamus" for a full explanation.) **Their capstone is the eye of Lucifer or Satan**. It is definitely not the all-seeing eye of Almighty God. Read the Latin words both above and below the pyramid.

Annuit Coeptis (Announcing the birth of) Novus Ordo Seclorum (A **secular**, heathenistic new order.)

A Filthy Usurper

Lucifer (Satan) is a foul creature, created by God for a special task in Heaven. Through his beauty and his wisdom, he fell through pride. He now has the audacity to endeavour to dethrone the true capstone of history.

JESUS CHRIST
THE TRUE CORNERSTONE
RIGHT ON THE TOP

24. If you look up to the top or apex of the pyramid, there is a little flat area there, awaiting the missing capstone. Let's identify Him from the prophecies.

"Wherefore also, it is contained in the Scripture, Behold, I lay in Sion **a chief corner-stone***, elect, precious, and he that believeth on Him shall not be confounded.*

Unto you therefore, which believe, He is precious, but unto them which be disobedient, the stone which the builders disallowed, the same is made **the head of the corner***."*[2] End quote.

There are other references, but this one is enough to establish the identity of the true capstone.

25. As we look at the top of the Great Pyramid as it is today (1998), we see the four corners very clearly. We are told that when Christ formed His true church, it was built upon a foundation of apostles and prophets. Ascending in the form of a pyramid, therefore, **Jesus Christ Himself is the chief corner-stone, and at his return, caps off the whole of history**.

Thus, the corner-stone is not at the base of the structure as we have been led to believe, but **right at the top**. He, the Lord Jesus Christ, will return shortly and lock all history together. **He is the divine 'lynch pin'.** **"King of Kings and Lord of Lords!"**

A Thrilling Discovery

During the month of April 1998, we were speaking at a Samoan camp in the Auckland area of New Zealand.

I was approaching the end of the lecture, and requested that we read the passage 1 Peter 2:7 from the Samoan Bible. At the risk of being accused of presenting irrelevant information, I herewith emphasise the latter portion of the verse.

"O le ma'a na lafoa'iina e tufaga fai fale ua avea lava lea ma tulimanu aupitoaluga." End quote.

The literal translation of this is *"**The stone which was rejected by the builders, it has become the corner at the absolute top**."*

As a boy, my old teachers taught me that the cornerstone was always placed first of all at the bottom corner of the structure. In this case, however, the Lord Jesus Christ is the chief cornerstone.

Please take careful note that the translators got it correctly from the original Greek, as they translated it into the Samoan language. Thus, **in this case, the Samoan translation is better than the English one.**

Jesus Christ, the Lord, will return after an absence from the earth of approximately 2000 years (2 days in His eyes), He will grab Lucifer by the throat, and remove him from the position of capstone of all history, throw him into Hell, and take his place.

Jesus Christ is the true capstone of history!

FOOTNOTES

[1] Isaiah 19:19-20

[2] 1 Peter 2:6-7

CHAPTER TWENTY-FIVE

THE COMPLETED JIGSAW

A headline in the Christchurch 'Press', 24th December 1983, is now going brown with age. It sits in a drawer in my desk and will probably still be there, even when I have passed on. It reads thus - *"Train Tragedy's 30th Anniversary.*

On Christmas morning about 1 a.m., when most of the 190 passengers will probably be asleep, the northbound train 626 will slow as it crosses the bridge spanning the Whangaehu River.

The locomotive driver will send a wreath spiralling into the river's placid waters, a ritual carried out on each of the 30 Christmases since New Zealand's worst railway disaster.

What happened at 10:21 p.m. on Thursday, December 24 1953?...

The railway bridge was thrust aside by a lahar, a huge outpour of water that had burst from Mount Ruapehu's crater lake, and now the 130-tonne, steam-driven, KA locomotive, hurtled headlong into the swollen river, dragging five of its nine carriages behind it, and leaving a sixth teetering on the brink.

...Of the 285 on board, 151 died." End quote.

One of the first bodies discovered by the searchers was that of my friend, Alan Drown. The night before, we had sat together in a motor car, until the early hours of the morning discussing our plans for the future.

The events that took place that fateful night ensured that neither Alan nor I fulfilled the plans we had for our lives.

He was gone. I was still here. My father came to my room early the next morning with the shattering news. I ran down the concrete steps and into the garage where my dad parked his car. Falling on my knees, through my tears, I cried out to the Lord to come into my life and to change me.

He did!

My prayer in those days of terrible crisis was not very professional, yet the Lord heard it. Since that morning, on Christmas Day 1953, my life has changed in many wonderful ways. Because of my foolish, stubborn ways, it took a **crisis**.

I pray that you, the reader, will not require a sudden tragedy such as I experienced to bring you to your knees.

Some readers at this point may rebel and say to themselves, "I will never have a crisis like this!" Yes, you will. I will personally guarantee that the following problems will affect you, sooner or later.

A) The death of somebody in your family, or somebody close to you.
B) A monetary problem, certainly by the end of 1999.
C) A food shortage problem, about the same time.
D) Sickness and no insurance cover.
E) Your own death.

Some, if not all of these things will affect you personally in the very near future.

Reading this book has caused you to understand your precarious position in the midst of a changing world. As your understanding increases, you may feel like a ship coming out from under a wave - shuddering, and finally bursting free.

Gradually, slowly, steadily, you now can see, the whole world system has been manipulated and changed. Most restructuring worked along the three-pronged attack system.

1. Leak it
2. Deny it
3. Do it

We've watched small businesses being decimated, as big businesses merge, merge, merge, until about six companies will control each country on earth.

The Problem

I hope by now, you realise that **the author of this confusion is the eye in the triangle** found on the reverse side of every $US1 bill. Therefore, **the problem is not political, religious, or economic, but spiritual.**

A spiritual problem requires a spiritual answer.

Jesus Christ made the answer very clear. *"You must be born again."*

We have all been born once, that is so obvious. To enter Heaven, however, we need a second birth. *"That which is born of the flesh is flesh. That which is born of the spirit is spirit."*[1]

My Questions to You

	Yes	No
1. Have you been born again?	☐	☐
2. Do you want to be?	☐	☐

God's Word promises that all is not doom and gloom however. Listen to a very significant prophetic word. *"...When the enemy shall come in like a flood, the Spirit of the Lord shall lift up a standard against him."*[2]

As we travel the world, teaching the tens of thousands who come to listen, many disillusioned people are finding hope and a new reason for living. I invite you right now, to humble yourself before the Lord, and get ready to pray **the sinner's prayer**.

A Covenant Agreement

How many people are involved in a covenant? Two or more.

In this case, it's the Lord and the sinner.

Jesus prayed His part of the covenant from the cross as He shed His precious blood on your behalf. *"Father, forgive them for they know not what they do."*[3]

Your Covenant Prayer

Part One

(Say out loud;

"Lord Jesus Christ - I come to you now - because I am a sinner.
Today Lord Jesus - I repent of my sin - I turn away from my sin - and I turn to you."

Part Two

"**I believe, dear Lord - that you died for me.** I (insert your name here).......................thank you Lord - because your blood covers all my sins. No one else can save me - only Jesus."

Part Three

"Right now - I open the door of my heart (put your hand to your chest and open outwards) - Come into my heart, Lord Jesus - Wash me - Cleanse me - and make me your child - I receive you now by faith.

Help me to live for you every day until you come again. I close the door (use your hand again and bring it back towards your chest) and you are on the inside.

I thank you, Lord Jesus, because today, by faith, I have received you - and you have received me."

Amen."

Here is the Promise

"...To as many (anybody) *as **received** Him* (Jesus), *to them gave He power to become the Sons of God..."*[4] (Emphasis added.)

Your choice today gives you that power, and right, to call yourself a Son of God. Praise Him now in your own words.

In order that you may never forget this great day, I include here a copy of your New Birth Certificate.

New Birth Certificate

At (time)...............................on (date)..

I (name)..

received the Lord Jesus Christ as my own Saviour.

I thank Him.

Signed:...

If you filled out this Certificate, please:

1. Copy it out again into the front page of your Bible;
2. Send another copy to me immediately, so that I can send you further assistance;
3. Go and tell someone what you have done.

"That if thou shalt confess with thy MOUTH, the Lord Jesus, and shalt believe in thine HEART that God has raised Him from the dead, thou shalt be saved."[5] End quote (Emphasis added).

That which is in your heart must come out of your mouth. This is your starting point.

Now: Steps to help you continue on for Christ -

1. Pray daily.
2. Read your Bible daily. Start in John's Gospel because it speaks about salvation and everlasting life.
3. Witness, or tell others about Christ.
4. Link up with a Bible-based Christian group or Church. (I may be able to help you here as I have friends in many different groups and denominations.)

Welcome to the family of God. I look forward to meeting you up there.

Your friend

Barry Smith

Footnotes

[1] John 3:6

[2] Isaiah 59:19   [4] John 1:12

[3] Luke 23:34   [5] Romans 10:9